4Life

God's Values for Living

4Life 2006

Many thanks to those at St Mary's Church, especially Paul Harwood, Alex Shuttle-worth, Rev. Richard Williams and Pippa Goldring. Thanks to Trevor Withers for giving me a chance and to Liz West for all her help with the final text. Thanks to the incomparable Ailsa. Thanks, too, to all those whose stories I have used, though names have been changed in each case.

4Life is based on The Arrival Kit by Ralph Neighbour (Cell UK, 1993, 1999 & 2000) and Deeper by Gabriel Smy (Cell UK 2003).

Cover design by **bluepig**design, Harlow, Essex

Published by:
Cell UK Ministries, Highfield Oval, Harpenden, Herts. AL5 4BX
Registered Charity No. 1088578

ISBN 1-902144-25-2   E&OE

Contents

Contents

Introducing
4Life

4Life is an introduction to a different way of living. It's about reaching the last page of this book and finding you've been changed by the experience. The ingredients are simple: 10 readings on your own, then a meeting with someone. 40 readings and 4 meetings in all - you could do it in 8 weeks. Or you could start beginners' Spanish. Or go jogging. Or catch up with the soaps. The choice is yours. But the invitation comes from none other than Jesus Christ: 'Let anyone who is thirsty come to me' (John 7:37). So what will it be? Do you want to know what's Spanish for bathroom, get cramp, or find out who shot Terry's mum? Or are you thirsty with the thirst that only followers of Jesus ever truly satisfy?

Why 4Life?

Have you ever been in a taxi driven by a total novice who's never been in a car before and only picked up some driving tips by flicking through Auto Weekly? ('I have!' you're thinking, 'I have!' - that's taxis for you). Realistically, though, no one ever learnt to drive like that. Advanced skills like driving are only picked up by people who invest the time to learn things at first-hand.

It's a bit like that with Christianity. Some people might think that you can inherit Christianity, or be vaccinated by it as a child. But you can't just sign up for it, like some heavenly insurance policy. It's not even enough to stock up with it on a weekly basis, like a shopper at Tesco. Jesus wasn't after consumers, badge-wearers or names on a list. He was after disciples – followers who were ready to learn from him and be changed by the experience. How about being one of them?

4Life is a guide to living as a disciple of Jesus Christ. It's written with spaces for you to record your reactions as you go through it. It's designed around 4 meetings with someone else - a sponsor - because on the whole we learn best one to one. And it's written in the hope that you can be part of a caring small group, or cell, because disciples need each other.

May God bless you as you work through 4Life,

Mark Powley

How it Works

To complete 4Life you will need:

- a pen
- a sponsor (another Christian to do 4Life with)
- a Bible (sometimes)
- a regular slot of about 15 minutes to complete each reading. Try to do no more than one reading per day. This will help you avoid spiritual indigestion!
- a meeting with your sponsor after every 10 readings, for about an hour. This could be four meetings over 8 weeks, or longer if you choose.

4Life has four sections which are the building blocks of the Christian life:

1 Identity (Who am I?) - Finding who you are as a Christian

2 Values (What's important?) - Facing what drives you

3 Lifestyle (How should we live?) - Forming new habits and losing old ones

4 Purpose (What can I do?) - Fulfilling God's plans for your life

If you're new to Christianity, you might need to concentrate especially on the first sections. Don't worry if not everything makes sense immediately. You can use the 4 meetings as a chance to raise questions as they come to you.

If you're more experienced and perhaps working with this material with a view to helping a newer Christian, you may feel you've covered some of the early material before, but bear with it. 4Life isn't mainly about passing on information; it's about letting your life be changed as the teachings of Jesus go to work deep inside you. What you write in this book will be as important as what you read. As you answer the questions honestly, the foundations of your life will be exposed and God can speak to you through the Bible and the time with your sponsor. Consider 4Life as a buildings inspection on your faith - it's always good to check that foundations are sound and deal with any underlying problems. As the units progress, God will certainly bring up things for you to focus on and which need your attention.

Choosing a Sponsor

Doing 4Life on your own would be like playing tennis against a wall. Find someone to meet with you after each section to discuss the units you've worked through and pray together. Ideally this would be a Christian who seems to be a few steps ahead of you, and someone who has worked through 4Life themselves. If you can't do this, you could try working through it both for the first time together. If you're really keen to benefit from the experience, you could have 8 Meetings - one after each 5 readings

Why Write Answers?

Writing answers is about being active as you learn. It's proven to help people remember things they've been studying. Writing will also allow you to make the most of the personal questions in the guide, and have something to discuss at each meeting.

Why Memorise Bible Verses?

You'll find a verse to memorise at the start of each unit. This isn't a return to 19th century schooling. It's about storing away important words so they can always be with us. We do this naturally with song words, passwords and wise proverbs. Advertisers, too, know how to stash away their message somewhere in our brain. But knowing you can do it when you B & Q it, or that L'Oreal is because you're worth it, or any other shallow nonsense isn't as important as knowing the truths God has inspired in the Bible. Which is why he asks us to stash away some of them in our brains along with everything else.

You can memorise a verse by simply saying it out loud over and over again. Memory verses work best when they're put in a rhythm, set to a tune, or linked with something else we remember. If you're the rebellious type, don't memorize the four main Bible verses. Instead, pick your own! The key thing is to learn the words of scripture, one way or another.

Closer to God

Each unit ends with a time to pray, and it will help to find some quiet space for this. This isn't an added extra but a vital part of 4Life. It's where you'll learn the lessons of prayer direct from the Master himself, and where the spiritual rubber starts to hit the road. 4Life uses the words and prayers of many different Christians throughout history. This will help you put down roots into the wisdom of all those who've gone before.

A Word to Leaders

What makes 4Life different to your average book on Christian basics?
4Life aims to be much more than just a pack of information to give a new or keen Christian, as if simply knowing more things would change their life. The idea is to encourage what is really needed:

- first-hand experience of being a disciple of Jesus
- a habit of personal devotion
- involvement in a small group
- a relationship with a mentor
- a change of mindset

- the practical skills of following Jesus

Tracy Cotterell from the London Institute of Contemporary Christianity has written, 'In our churches today, we generally have a teaching culture rather than an active learning culture that models apprenticeship... We have to be 'intentional' about passing on skills in faith'.

4Life is written to do just that. It's designed:

- to encourage daily interaction between Jesus and the reader
- to facilitate the relationship between a Christian and their mentor
- to be interactive, with space for each individual's different issues to be addressed
- to be broad enough to be used in churches of many types

Probably most important of all, it zeros in on our values - the unspoken assumptions that affect our day to day choices (see the Values section). In this way it encourages a wholesale change of mentality - from modern day consumer to disciple of Jesus Christ.

All these features make 4Life suitable not just for new or young Christians, but also for any Christian who would like to be mentored, or to learn the lifestyle of a committed cell group, or to review the values that shape their life.

In a church situation, you may want to ask certain mature Christians to do 4Life themselves first. They can then be on hand when the time comes to make 4Life available to other church members. The main thing, as the Sponsor's Guide explains (p. 102), is that 4Life is driven by the person doing it.

Finding your way round the Bible (If you're new to it)

The Bible is made up of 66 books, each split into chapters and smaller sentences (verses). The first 39 books, the Old Testament, come from the time before Jesus was born. The last 27 books, the New Testament, were written after Jesus. In this book, a reference like John 3:16 refers to the book of John (which is in the New Testament) chapter 3 and the 16th verse (often shown by little numbers). In 4Life all the Bible verses are taken from Today's New International Version. If you can, make sure you have a readable translation of the Bible to hand when it comes to looking up verses yourself.

The books in the Bible break down like this:

The Old Testament

The Law *(including early stories of God's people)* Genesis, Exodus, Leviticus, Numbers, Deuteronomy

Old Testament History *(the story of the nation Israel)* Joshua, Judges, Ruth, 1 Samuel, 2 Samuel, 1 Kings, 2 Kings, 1 Chronicles, 2 Chronicles, Ezra, Nehemiah, Esther

Poetry & wisdom *(a collection of wise sayings, poems and prayers)* Job, Psalms, Proverbs, Ecclesiastes, Song of Songs

The Prophets *(messages to God's people)* Isaiah, Jeremiah, Lamentations, Ezekiel, Daniel, Hosea, Joel, Amos, Obadiah, Jonah, Micah, Nahum, Habakkuk, Zephaniah, Haggai, Zechariah, Malachi

The New Testament

New Testament History *(including the four gospels, telling Jesus' life story)* Matthew, Mark, Luke, John, Acts

The Letters *(written to early Christians)* Romans, 1 Corinthians, 2 Corinthians, Galatians, Ephesians, Philippians, Colossians, 1 Thessalonians, 2 Thessalonians, 1 Timothy, 2 Timothy, Titus, Philemon, Hebrews, James, 1 Peter, 2 Peter, 1 John, 2 John, 3 John, Jude

New Testament Prophecy *(a vision to encourage early churches)* Revelation

The journey begins

'Map?' 'Check'
'Compass?' 'Check'
'Kendal mint cake?' 'Check.
Let's go'
'Hold on, do we even know where we're going?!'

Before we trek through all the essentials of Christian living, it's probably worth checking that we know where we're going. In a culture where a cross can be just another form of necklace, we need to check we've got our ideas straight. And who else can point us in the right direction but Jesus Christ himself?

God Has Come Near

> ...Jesus went into Galilee, proclaiming the good news of God. "The time has come," he said. "The kingdom of God has come near. Repent and believe the good news!"
> **Mark 1:14-15**

When Jesus walked around Palestine 2,000 years ago, he announced that God was coming near. The God of Christianity isn't a distant deity, forever shrouded behind the clouds. God hasn't left himself to be discussed on late night chat shows and exploited by religious salesmen. He has come near.

In Jesus, God has stepped into history. And when he did, he began a new state of affairs: the kingdom of God. God's kingdom is his vision for the world. It's a powerful new reality where God's will is done. It can turn people's lives upside down, heal them, forgive them and reconnect them with their loving Maker. For two thousand years the kingdom of God has been the greatest force in human history, and right now its powers and possibilities are open to me and you.

Our Response

God has come near - that's his part. What about us?

What did Jesus tell people to do?

Repent & believe.
Love one another

Look again at the verses in Mark 1. To repent is to change your mind and your life. To believe means to put your trust in Jesus. Imagine you're sailing a yacht in the middle of the ocean. Suddenly you receive a storm warning from the coastguard and a new course for you to sale. In that situation, you'd need to *repent* of your current course and have *faith* in the coastguard as the one who can save you.

Becoming a Christian is just like this. The Bible tells us that we're on the wrong course. We are living for ourselves instead of living for God and for others. This deep-seated selfishness cuts us off from God and leads us into godless and hopeless lifestyles. A storm warning like this can be hard to hear. But the One who gave it also had a rescue plan at his own expense.

God's rescue plan was to come and save us himself, by sending Jesus Christ. Through Jesus, God reestablished contact with us. He showed us a new way to live. And he dealt with sin – the selfishness that keeps us from God – by dying for us on a cross. Now the way is open. We can reconnect with God, in a deep and loving relationship, and we can chart a new course for a life of love modelled on Jesus. Our rescue begins when we say sorry to God and choose to begin a new life with him.

✎ **Which of these actually makes someone a Christian:**

☐ Care for the poor and needy
☐ Start over again as a follower of Jesus
☐ Understand the meaning of the Bible
☐ Be a committed church member
☐ Pray honestly and regularly
☑ Trust in Jesus Christ

A Christian should do all of these things, but what actually *makes* someone a Christian is repentance and faith (the second and last options). Repentance and faith make us Christians before we ever do any good deeds and they keep us close to God through the whole journey, too.

A New Start

It should be clear by now that Christianity is all about making a new start. This may be hard for us to accept because we often feel we have life under control. But there's a choice about Jesus Christ that we each need to make for ourselves. Will we accept his call to repent? This means recognizing our basic selfishness and owning up to the fact that we need God's help to change. Will we accept his call to believe? This means acknowledging that Jesus is

God's Son, the One who came to save us, and committing ourselves totally to him and the new way of life in his kingdom.

Jesus said that following him was the ultimate new beginning, like being born all over again (John 3:3). It may be costly, but it's the doorway to a new life, and a new relationship with God as a loving Father. That's why many millions of people have found that the new start offered by Jesus rings with the most beautiful music imaginable. It's good news for everyone who realises that they need God. And it was good news to me when, as an 18 year-old, I made my own decision (one of many) to start again with God. I've never looked back.

What's your reaction to Jesus' offer?

✎ **Have you taken the step of repentance and faith in Jesus?**

☐ No, not yet
☐ I'm not sure
☐ I can't pinpoint a moment, but I know deep down that I have
☐ Yes

Do you know when? _____

☐ Yes, but I need to renew my choice again

☐ No, but I want to start today

What about Baptism?

From the earliest times, people who chose to follow Jesus for the first time have been baptised. Baptism is about washing away the old life and coming out of the water into a new life as part of the people of God. In the first sermon ever given by the early church, Peter, one of Jesus' followers, explained: "Repent and be baptized, every one of you, in the name of Jesus Christ for the forgiveness of your sins. And you will receive the gift of the Holy Spirit..." (Acts 2:37-38).

God works powerfully through baptism to mark us out as his forgiven people. It's a vital symbol of the death of our old, self-reliant and rebellious life, and the beginning of a life spent following Jesus.

If you haven't been baptised, you'll need to consider doing so. If you have, that baptism is the true mark of your identity and something to remember for life.

⧗ Closer to God

Be honest with God - have you made a new start and begun to trust in Jesus?
You could use this prayer now.

Heavenly Father, I am sorry for the things I have done wrong in my life (take a few moments to ask his forgiveness for anything particular that is on your conscience).

Please forgive me. I now turn from everything which I know is wrong.

Thank you that you sent your Son, Jesus, to die on the cross for me so that I could be forgiven and set free. From now on I will follow and obey him as my Lord.

Thank you that you offer me this gift of forgiveness and your Spirit. I now receive that gift.

Please come into my life by your Holy Spirit to be with me forever.

Through Jesus Christ, our Lord. Amen.

Nicky Gumbel

Identity

See what great love the Father has lavished on us,
that we should be called children of God!
And that is what we are!

1 John 3:1

'If you could ask God just one question, what would it be?' This is what a rough group of bikers were asked late one night in an Australian pub. Eventually an old Vietnam veteran spoke up, **'Who am I?'**.

Our true identity is one of the most important things we can find out. If we knew the truth about who we are, we'd be astounded. Who we really are, though, not who others think we are or what the TV says about us. The Christian journey begins with our identity. Unless we know it we cannot get started; once we know it, nothing will be able to stop us.

A New Teacher

Some people want to learn, others don't. When I worked as a teacher, I began to pick up the telltale signs that pupils were beginning to switch off: glazed eyes, secretly listening to music, climbing out of the window, walking round the classroom wearing car headrests as slippers... (I'm not kidding!). Many of us weren't brought up to pay attention to Jesus, either. At least, not as a competent guide for life. But what would happen if we did?

We may think of Jesus in many ways: a hero, a great leader, our saviour, friend, even the Son of God. But what interested Jesus most wasn't fans, sympathizers, or even just worshippers. He was looking for disciples – students who would follow in his steps and learn his lifestyle. That's why he spent so much of his time choosing disciples, training them personally, and instructing them to call others.

When we repent and believe the good news about Jesus (see The Journey Begins) we are saved from living and dying without God. But this isn't all of it. Jesus also leads us into a new kind of life following him, the life we were made for. As Dallas Willard has said, 'the really good news for humanity is that Jesus is now taking students in the master class of life'.

Rock Solid Living

Here's Jesus' own summary of the effects of becoming his student, his prospectus for the school of discipleship:

"Therefore everyone who hears these words of mine and puts them into practice is like a wise man who built his house on the rock. The rain came down, the streams rose, and the winds blew and beat against that house; yet it did not fall, because it had its foundation on the rock. But everyone who hears these words of mine and does not put them into practice is like a foolish man who built his house on sand. The rain came down, the streams rose, and the winds blew and beat against that house, and it fell with a great crash." **Matthew 7:24-27**

What is the key to living through the storms of life?

How willing are you to learn new things as a disciple of Jesus?

4Life - The Curriculum

4Life seeks to learn from Jesus in 4 key areas:

Identity

In a world that promises to tell us who we are by our job, our ethnic group, the music we like, or the things we buy, Jesus offers a different identity. This isn't another lifestyle option to buy into or a self-change package, it's about discovering our true identity - who we were made to be. Without Jesus we'd be stuck in a meaningless world, living behind masks. But thanks to him we've been brought back to God as dearly loved children. There's never been news like this.

See what great love the Father has lavished on us, that we should be called children of God! And that is what we are! **1 John 3:1**

A New Teacher

Values

We all have deeply held values and beliefs that we live by. Have any of these statements ever influenced the way you think?

- [ ] Life's just a game
- [x] We should look after number one
- [ ] Family always comes first
- [ ] The universe has no meaning
- [ ] The most important thing about me is my ethnicity / sexuality / income / success
- [ ] The key thing is a comfortable life

These ideas and others like them affect the way all of us think and make our choices. But Jesus had some ideas of his own: 'seek first the kingdom of God'; 'love God with all your heart'; and 'love your neighbour as yourself'. To know the words he said is one thing; but to let the meaning change you is another. It's the work of a lifetime, but it gets serious attention in the Values section.

Lifestyle

A Christian without a godly lifestyle is like electrical gear from a dodgy market stall - shiny on the outside, with all the right labels, but practically useless. God's plan for us is so much greater than this: a life of love, joy, peace, and more. How do we drop the habits that drag us down and pick up healthy Christian disciplines that will change us from the inside out? This is the focus of the Lifestyle section.

Can you identify habits you would like to drop? Yes!

Purpose

How would you describe the purpose of your life?

That's a question you don't get in your average pub quiz! Or many other places, for that matter. But few questions are more important. You may have a clear idea already; you may not. Either way, Jesus had a lot to say on the issue. Like any carpenter recruiting apprentices to help fit out a house, Jesus calls disciples to work with him to heal and save the world. How about it?

Turning Words Into Action

As with any master class, the information in 4Life is only useful if it's lived out. Just quietly reading the sessions won't make the difference. The key is to turn words into action: to pray, to talk with your sponsor, to make choices and begin to live differently. This is the aim of 4Life: to put into practice the words of the greatest Teacher of all. It may feel slow at first, and difficult in places, but stick with it - the lessons taught by Jesus and his followers can't be truly learnt in any other way. Are you ready to begin?

⧗ Closer to God

Behold, behold,
I make all things new
Beginning with you
And starting from today

Behold, behold,
I make all things new
My promise is true
For I am Christ the Way

From Revelation 21:5
John Bell (The Iona Community)

IDENTITY 2

A New Life

**How can I be sure that I'm a Christian?
How can I be sure God is there at all?
Has my life really changed?**
Questions like these have been on the minds of Christians since the very beginning.

How sure are you that you're really a Christian?

change

John, one of Jesus' disciples, wrote this to the early church:

> Everyone who believes that Jesus is the Messiah is born of God, and everyone who loves the father loves his child as well. This is how we know that we are the children of God: by loving God and carrying out his commands. In fact, this is love for God: to obey his commands. And his commands are not burdensome, for everyone born of God overcomes the world. ...I write these things to you who believe in the name of the Son of God so that you may know that you have eternal life.   **1 John 5:1-5, 13**

John wrote to these early Christians to end the uncertainty. He wrote 'so that you may know that you have eternal life'. He wanted them to be **sure** of the new identity they had been given. So what makes a genuine Christian? You need to believe that Jesus is more than just a helpful man in history - he's 'the Messiah' (God's chosen King and rescue plan for humanity) and 'the Son of God' (God himself in human form). This is the key, says John: a relationship of trust with Jesus. Christians still struggle with selfishness, still have doubts, still fail. The difference is that they've put their trust in Jesus Christ.

So Christians still struggle, but that doesn't mean they just stay the same. John explains that disciples of Jesus discover a new love for God and for others. Following God seems less of a burden, too. These are all signs that God is at work. They show that he's working in your life to overcome your selfishness, and that he'll rescue you from death, too. This is what the Bible means by 'eternal life' – a new life with God that starts now and will go on beyond death into eternity.

How has being a Christian changed your life?

Vital Signs

What signs can you see in your life?
- [ ] A more sensitive conscience
- [ ] Talking to God through the day
- [ ] A new love for people around me
- [ ] A deep sense of God's love for me
- [ ] A feeling that I've been forgiven
- [ ] Wanting to read the Bible more
- [ ] A desire to praise God
- [ ] Leaving old selfish habits behind
- [ ] Wanting to obey Jesus and be more like him
- [ ] Powerful signs such as miracles or a new prayer language (see Purpose 2)
- [ ] Past hurts being healed

You may not have all these signs, but new Christians will start to see several of them. If you're sure you don't have any, talk about it with your sponsor and perhaps go back to The Journey Begins (p. 10).

A New Life

The signs of faith can't be faked or whipped up. They grow naturally. As Jesus said, a good tree just can't help producing good fruit (Luke 6:43). God has given you new life and it will bear fruit in time. Right now his power is at work, changing you from the inside out. As this happens, the vital signs of Christian faith will blossom and bloom in you. You'll be able to see it, and so will the people around you.

But, as any gardener will tell you, growth takes patience and being willing to get your hands dirty! God is like that with us, tirelessly sticking with us through our ups and downs. But he promises to produce good things in us as surely as summer follows spring.

📖 God's Life in You

Have a look at these Bible passages:
Who lives in you?
1 Corinthians 3:16

God's Spirit

What was Paul confident of?
Philippians 1:6

That what has been started shall be completed.

Who works in us and why?
Philippians 2:12-13

God - to carry out his purpose.

It seems incredible, doesn't it? God himself is actually living in you. But it's true. Your job isn't to make everything happen, but to learn to recognize the way God works and simply co-operate with him.

Dealing with the wobbles

At every stage of faith, from new Christian to mature believer, the biggest threats to feeling sure are the 2 d's: doubts and disasters. Doubts will rise in your mind as you step out to follow Jesus. And disasters will certainly happen, whether it's hassle from others, your own mistakes, or just things going wrong. None of this means you're not really a Christian. In fact, it shows your faith is real - its a real risk (so it's natural to sometimes feel doubtful) and its a real change (which is why you'll face opposition from others and from the devil).

Remember, too, that having doubts is part of growing in faith. Ask any teacher: no one ever learnt anything without asking questions.

Even feeling guilty after we do something selfish is a positive sign - it means that God's Spirit is still in us, convicting us about sin (John 16:8). Many times I've knelt by my bed close to tears and clung to the promise earlier in John's letter:

> If we claim to be without sin, we deceive ourselves and the truth is not in us. If we confess our sins, he is faithful and just and will forgive us our sins and purify us from all unrighteousness.
>
> **1 John 1:8-9**

Do you remember learning to ride a bike? The key (just in case you're still learning) is to keep pedaling. Faith is the same. When the wobbles come, keep going, and you'll find God is still at work, supporting you and teaching you to ride out the bumps with him.

⏳ Closer to God

Look back at the Vital Signs list and spend some time thanking God for his work in your life. Also, think about the memory verse on page 13. Thank God for what it says and commit it to memory (see the tips on p.7) so it can always encourage you.

A New Family

Anyone who's ever shared a house knows that living in a family is difficult. So many people but only one remote control! And yet, we humans still belong in families. Even if it's not our blood-relations, we long to be loved and accepted for who we are, to have people who stick by us through thick and thin. So it shouldn't surprise us that God has planned from the beginning to make us part of a family. At first God called one man, Abraham, to start a family that would know him (see Genesis 12:1-3), and this family became the Jewish nation. Then Jesus, one of Abraham's descendants, called people from every nation to join the people of God. Jesus said, 'Whoever does the will of my Father in heaven is my brother and sister and mother' (Matthew 12:50). If you're a Christian, you're part of Jesus' family, and God is your Father.

What is church?

You might think of church as a building – maybe one on a street near you – but 'church' is actually the name for a gathered group of people. We still call the buildings churches, but church in the Bible is like a family or a household. Look at what the apostle Paul wrote to some new Christians:

> Consequently, you are no longer foreigners and strangers, but fellow citizens with God's people and also members of God's household, built on the foundation of the apostles and prophets, with Christ Jesus himself as the chief corner-stone.　**Ephesians 2:19-20**

Instead of being 'strangers' to God's family, these new Christians are now 'members of God's household'. To be a Christian is to be included in a huge family: it stretches right back through the ages, to Abraham, and it stretches round the world to include millions of brothers and sisters, whoever believes and trusts in Jesus as God's Son. Building on Jesus, and the faithful 'apostles and prophets' like Paul who passed on his teaching, God is putting something together which is much greater than the sum of its parts.

There are no first or second class members in God's household, we're all 'fellow citizens'. That counts for you, whatever your background, whatever your appearance, whatever your personality and whatever your past experience has been. The church is no factory for clones; it's a place of diversity, a house of grace with the space for every kind of person to find who they were made to be.

Re-learning Church

✐ **What's your experience of church?**

☐ A friendly club
☐ A distant organisation
☐ A committed family
☐ A bunch of hypocrites
☐ Other: A reflexion of the world – good & sometimes bad.

You could be forgiven for any one of the reactions in this list. But Jesus definitely intended his followers to be a committed family. The church just hasn't always lived up to this calling. That's why it's important to re-learn what church is all about.

A New Family

So what do we find if we return to our roots? We find that Jesus didn't only speak to crowds; he also gathered around him a close-knit group of disciples. After his death and resurrection, they kept the same balance: meeting regularly in large gatherings, but also in small groups. 'Every day they continued to meet together in the temple courts. They broke bread in their homes and ate together with glad and sincere hearts' (Acts 2:46).

Modern groups called 'cells' have caught the same flame which set these early groups alight. Instead of simply attending big meetings, cells bring us together in little families where we can grow in faith, share each other's lives and reach out to others. The earliest groups of Christians multiplied and grew right across the Roman world. In the same way, like the cells in our bodies, cell groups also aim to grow by multiplying.

If we're going be re-learn what church is about, some popular ideas might need to go.

✐ Which ideas have you sometimes believed?

☐ Faith is a private, personal business
☐ Christianity is all about receiving
☐ Needing others is a sign of weakness
☐ If I'm honest, people will reject me
☐ Some people could never belong as part of God's family

Despite what some might say, there's simply no such thing as solo-Christianity - we need each other. This is God's plan: to draw us together in groups where we truly support each other, grow as Christians and multiply. If you can't join a group like this, then maybe you should find one or start one!

No Spectators

A football match with 40,000 players and no spectators would be pretty chaotic. But 40,000 spectators and no players at all would be worse! Mercifully, in God's family there's room for everyone to take part. That's the genius of cell groups - there are so many ways to be involved, whether it's contributing to discussions, praying, hosting, helping, inviting others, leading part of a meeting or leading the group.

How involved are you in your cell?

Spectator   Player

o   o   ●   o   o   o   o   o   o

How could you get more involved?

-Pray more
- Socialise more

However involved you are right now, there's a place for you in God's family. Somehow God will put you with other Christians, and he'll use the group to change all of your lives forever.

⏳ Closer to God

In the space below write the names of the people in your cell or small group.

Wendy + Ed   Navinda
Mike & Kay
Alan
Martin & Joanna
Catherine & Ian

Pray for God to bless each one and tell him anything you know they need.

New Beginnings

Apparently learning to ski is more difficult than it looks. Normally well-balanced people find themselves wobbling around like toddlers. Of course, if they persevere, they'll end up gliding effortlessly through the snow. But try telling that to someone who's just fallen over for the 22nd time in half an hour.

You've probably guessed it: following Jesus is just like this. You could be greatly expert in your job, or brilliantly clever, or have many decades of life experience. But when it comes to following Jesus, you may be just a beginner. Jesus said, 'Unless you change and become like little children, you will never enter the kingdom of heaven' (Matthew 18:3). What did he mean? Well, think about being a child. I'm guessing that you didn't change your own nappies or teach yourself how to speak! Like all kids, you'd have needed help.

If you're a new Christian, this is exactly what's going on now. No matter what your physical age, spiritually you are very young, so there are things you're going to need to learn, and habits that will need to change. But older Christians, too, can have some growing up to do. Some Christians are very enthusiastic about the Bible but never share their faith; some have impressive gifts but lack a godly lifestyle; some have great passion but hurt others with their unloving attitude. Lastly, some Christians haven't really grown at all; all they have is the faith they grew up with or the fading memory of a conversion experience which never carried through to the rest of their life.

Which of these things apply to you and why?

Whatever stage we are at, growing in faith means a second childhood with all its new struggles, and new joys, too. Are you ready for that?

Growing Up

Anyone who lives on milk, being still an infant, is not acquainted with the teaching about righteousness. But solid food is for the mature, who by constant use have trained themselves to distinguish good from evil.
Hebrews 5:13-14

The mark of a 'mature' Christian isn't their age; it's the fact that they've trained themselves to tell good from evil. Over time, they have learnt the 'teaching about righteousness (right living)', but before that, they needed the baby milk of basic facts about Christianity. In our self-reliant culture, we might think we know all about what's right and wrong – but the Bible says otherwise. Our God-given consciences are under-developed, and like a toddler with scissors, trusting our instincts alone will cause more harm than good.

Suzie, a new Christian, had grown up with people who never taught her that lying was wrong. David and Jodie came to Christ while still experimenting with drugs and living together. Each of these people needed the humility to think again about what they'd assumed was right, as well as the patience to learn a new lifestyle.

New Beginnings

What areas might you need to review with your sponsor to enable you to grow?

Spiritual Parents

One way God teaches us is by the example of other mature Christians. These are spiritual parents. The apostle Paul was a spiritual parent to the Christians he wrote to here:

> . . .just as a nursing mother cares for her children, so we cared for you. Because we loved you so much, we were delighted to share with you not only the gospel of God but our lives as well... You are witnesses, and so is God, of how holy, righteous and blameless we were among you who believed. For you know that we dealt with each of you as a father deals with his own children, encouraging, comforting and urging you to live lives worthy of God, who calls you into his kingdom and glory.
>
> **1 Thessalonians 2:7-8, 10-12**

How was Paul like a mother with them?

Nurturing, spending time with, loving

How was he like a father?

Encouraging, comforting, urging

As we've seen, Christians are fellow citizens together - there are no big chiefs, we're all little Indians! But we can still learn from each other. Especially from Christians whose lives are so open to God that it shows.

Caught not taught

It so happens that, like a bad cold or a local accent, Christianity is caught and not just taught. That's how it spreads and always has been. One early Christian, Irenaeus, described how he learnt his faith from an old man called Polycarp, who learnt from John the disciple, who learnt from Jesus himself! Along with small groups, spiritual parents are vital to learning the faith at first-hand. What are the signs of being a spiritual parent? Paul mentions being loving, holy (pure) and encouraging. Another sign is having spiritual children – someone who has brought other people to the Lord.

Was anyone involved in introducing you to Jesus? Who?

(So you may know one parent already!)

Who else could be a spiritual parent for you?

How might you get to know them more?

Paul says 'we shared with you not only the gospel of God but our lives as well'. It's worth spending time with people who really seem to have caught Christianity, especially those in your cell. As you share each others' lives, Godly thinking, attitudes and behaviour *will* rub off.

⌛ Closer to God

Pray again for your cell. Also, ask God to show you who to consider as a spiritual parent.

He who walks with the wise grows wise
Proverbs 13:20

New Management

It's a familiar scene: the football club chairman faces a room flickering with photo flashes and gives the news. The manager he expressed 'full confidence' in last month has been sacked. Here at his side is the new manager. From now on there will be new tactics, new players and a new training regime. Everything will change.

The Call

> As Jesus walked beside the Sea of Galilee, he saw Simon and his brother Andrew casting a net into the lake, for they were fishermen. "Come, follow me," Jesus said, "and I will send you out to fish for people." At once they left their nets and followed him.
> **Mark 1:16-18**

Notice that Jesus didn't negotiate with his followers; he called them. This is why he's often called 'Lord' (the word means boss or manager). When Jesus called followers, he called them to follow him as their Lord, to put their lives under his management.

Whenever there's new management, there are changes. Simon and Andrew left their jobs to follow Jesus. They left behind their old way of life, risking their time, their income, and their place in the community. But what they gained was awesome: personal access to Jesus, full-time tuition from him, and first hand experience of God's love and power. On top of all this, Jesus gave them a new purpose. They would fish for people, gathering others to follow Jesus, too.

Think about this for a moment. Who has the authority to call people like this? Or make promises like this? Only God can demand our whole lives (because he gave them to us in the first place). Jesus isn't just one option in a marketplace of world faiths, he is God himself. To put your life under the management of Jesus is to put it under the management of God. This means living for him in every area of our lives (2 Corinthians 5:15).

In what areas are you living for yourself rather than for Jesus?

The Cost

Later in Mark's gospel, Jesus explains:

> Then he called the crowd to him along with his disciples and said: "Whoever wants to be my disciple must deny themselves and take up their cross and follow me. For whoever wants to save their life will lose it, but whoever loses their life for me and for the gospel will save it."
> **Mark 8:34-35**

What's the only way to save your life?

There's no softening the blow. To deny yourself means to consistently put the interests of God and others above your own. To take up your cross means to be willing to face suffering and rejection, even if it costs you your life. To follow Jesus means to make his priorities your priorities; his values your values; his attitude your attitude.

It doesn't sound an easy package! But then what's the alternative? Jesus doesn't call us because he wants to make life difficult. Quite the opposite - he loves us and wants to save our lives. He could leave us to live selfishly, shutting God out of the picture. But Jesus knows that road is a dead end: it only leads to more selfishness and judgment. Jesus' way is tough, but it's the way of love and it leads us back to God. In fact, it's only a life of love, reconnected to God that can make us truly happy anyway.

Denying yourself doesn't mean forgetting everything you are (after all, God made you). It means no longer putting yourself first, and trusting that God can still fulfill your life. As we'll see in later sections, this will mean a change of values and a change of lifestyle. And it has costs. David, who became a Christian as a teenager, was forced to leave home by his family's anger at his decision. This was the cost of discipleship. But despite this, David hung on as a Christian, his life was changed by God and he now has a family of his own. Even more important, Jesus has promised him eternal life.

Disciples of Jesus

Jesus called his followers 'disciples' which, means learners or apprentices. A Christian is someone who is constantly learning and constantly changing as they learn. To be a Christian is to be a student of Jesus, with him as your number one life coach. This is why the Bible is so important. The first part, the Old Testament, was honoured by Jesus as God's words. The second part, the New Testament, contains the only reliable accounts of his life and the inspired writings of his closest followers. As you read the Bible and try to follow its words, God will shape your life and you'll grow closer to the greatest Teacher of all.

What attracts you to following Jesus?

What makes it hard for you?

- ☑ How can I give up old habits?
- ☑ Can I trust God to look after me?
- ☑ Do I have time to learn all this?
- ☑ Can I trust the Bible?
- ☑ Will I understand everything?
- ☑ Will I be able to make sacrifices?
- ☐ Other:

Questions like these are natural, but none of them need to keep you from being a disciple. We each need to count the cost of following Jesus (Luke 14:25-33). But there's no cost like the cost he bore for us on the cross, and no benefit like the benefit of the new and everlasting life that he brings.

☒ Closer to God

Look back to the passages from Mark's gospel. Imagine Jesus calling you as if you were one of the first disciples.

> Thanks be to you, my Lord Jesus Christ,
> for all the blessings and benefits
> which you have given to me,
> for all the pains and insults
> you have borne for me.
> O most merciful Friend
> my Brother and Redeemer,
> may I know you more clearly,
> love you more dearly
> and follow you more nearly
> day by day
>
> *Richard of Chichester*

Wonderfully Made

A group of girls suffering from anorexia were asked to draw a life-size outline of their bodies against a wall. Then they stood against the wall for a photo. Around each girl was a huge outline, and somewhere inside the lines stood some-one a fraction of the size. Their self-image had been totally distorted.
The way you see yourself is absolutely crucial.

Write some words to describe yourself.

It's incredible how deeply our self-image affects us. Over time, despite the good experiences we may have, we all pick up negative views of ourselves. 'A failure', 'a mistake', 'an F-grade', 'arrogant', 'useless', 'ugly', 'not good enough'... These words can hang around at the back of our minds throughout our lives. People are driven by them, like unscratchable itches. One man, labeled 'sparrow legs' as a school kid, was still running marathons 20 years later to prove people wrong, even though no one was looking any more.

We all search for acceptance in different ways. Some of us try to earn ourselves a better label, like 'fashionable', 'strong', or 'successful'. Some of us push ourselves to the limit, or humiliate others in our quest for approval. Some of us collect achievements like trophies, or hoard possessions. Whatever makes us feel valuable - a successful job, a tidy home, a happy family...
Others of us try to run away. Perhaps we hide behind quietness, or starve ourselves into invisibility. We might try to lose ourselves in someone else's personality, or in endless good works. Or we simply blot out the pain with an addictive high.

Humans can't live without acceptance, but our desperate search for it drives us to some dangerous extremes. It's the effects of these extremes we'll be dealing with in later units.

Which of these has ever been a source of identity for you?

- [ ] I am what I own
- [ ] I am what I eat
- [ ] I am what I wear
- [ ] I am my sex life
- [ ] I am what I achieve or what I earn
- [ ] I am what others think
- [ ] I am someone because of the people I know or the group I belong to
- [ ] I am what I know
- [ ] I am what I control
- [ ] I am of no value at all

What effects has this had on your life?

None of us was meant to be reduced to the things in the list above. They are false identities; distorted mirrors which promise to give us a true identity but only twist us out of shape. In particular, we can be highly influenced by the views others have of us.

Wonderfully Made

Look at the words you wrote about yourself. Where did they come from?

Your True Identity

Do you know the only person who can authorize a UK passport? The Queen (check the front of one, if you don't believe me!). Christianity is the same: only Jesus the King can guarantee your true identity. Other people, no matter how well they know you, can only guess. Some of what they say or think is right, some is wrong; none of it is perfect. Only God, who sees everything, knows the full story. He knows you even better than you know yourself. Anything that doesn't match what he reveals about your identity is a lie. Are you ready to look in a true mirror - a mirror without any distortions?

> For you created my inmost being;
> you knit me together in my mother's womb.
> I praise you because I am fearfully and wonderfully made;
> your works are wonderful,
> I know that full well.   **Psalm 139:13-14**

What is good about you according to this Psalm?

What stops you thinking like this?

Here's a powerful truth: you were made by God. You are not an accident. You have been handmade by the loving and wise ruler of the universe, and his fingerprints are all over you. Like a Shakespeare play or Picasso canvas, you bear the marks of the master; your body, your personality and your gifts are the authentic work of God himself.

This doesn't make you perfect (I'm guessing that you know that already). But it does mean that who you really are, the very heart of what makes you 'you', is good. There is good in you that can never be erased, for God creates no fundamentally evil thing.

In fact, not only have we been made *by* God, we are *like* God - 'in his own image' (Genesis 1:27). We are creative, like God; responsible for the world, like God; spiritual beings capable of relationships, like God. This likeness has been spoiled by our selfishness (and by the evil done to us) but it remains - in you and in every person on earth.

Restoring the Image

There is of course another set of lies about us - that we're all gods, with the power to shape our own destiny. The Bible isn't fooled, though. 'All have sinned and fall short of the glory of God' (Romans 3:23). Humans aren't to be demonized, but we shouldn't be idolized either. We have been made in God's image, but we need to be saved and restored in a way that only our maker can do (see unit 10). But thankfully that's exactly what Jesus promises.

⧗ Closer to God

Spend some time praising God for how he has made you.

Also, thank him for all that you were made to be and that one day he'll restore you fully.

Extravagantly Loved

Being loved is the most amazing thing. The thrill of a first kiss, the reassuring squeeze of a friend's hug, a child running to their mum... There's no denying, we were made for love.

Now God doesn't always get a good press when it comes to love. But our yearning desire for love actually comes from him. God is the source of love. In fact, 'God IS love' (1 John 4:8). Love is God's nature; the word that describes him best.

Being so full of love, it shouldn't surprise us that God isn't a lonely figure, but a Trinity - three persons bound together in love. It's not perfect maths, but the Bible reveals that God is a mysterious unity of Father, Son and Holy Spirit (see Matthew 28:19) whose love for each other knows no limits.

From the beginning of the world, this love in God has overflowed to every creature on earth, and especially to God's people, Israel. Over the centuries, and despite their many failures, God showed them: 'I have loved you with an everlasting love' (Jeremiah 31:3). Eventually God's love drove him to pay the cost of forgiving all of us, even though it meant sending his Son to die for us. 'For God so loved the world that he gave his one and only Son, that whoever believes in him shall not perish but have eternal life' (John 3:16). That's how great God's love is.

Lies about God

A little like politicians, God is often seen in some pretty inaccurate cartoon-style ways. To some he's like a cosmic policeman. To others he's an absent father, or even a bearded old man in the sky.

🖉 **Which of these have you thought?**

☐ God is just a force in the universe
☐ God is impossible to please
☐ God is a harsh judge
☐ God couldn't really love me
☐ God is a made-up story
☐ God feels a million miles away
☐ God doesn't really care about evil

These old ideas can still affect us. You might feel guilty because deep down you still feel that God is out to get you. You might be busy trying to earn the approval of the harsh 'God' you grew up with. Or you could struggle to believe that God can come close to you at all.

Underline anything in the list above that might still influence you.

The Truth about God

Over time, God will teach you who he is. As you read the Bible, pray and walk with God in your life, you'll discover his true character. Here are some of God's awesome characteristics and verses where you can find out more.

- God is loving (Psalm 103:8-13, Romans 8:38-39)
- God is patient (2 Peter 3:9)
- God is just and fair (Deuteronomy 32:3-4)
- There's no evil in God (1 John 1:5)
- God is trustworthy (2 Timothy 2:11-13)
- God keeps his promises (Numbers 23:19)
- God provides (Psalm 111:4-9)

Extravagantly Loved

- God is generous (James 1:5)
- God is holy and pure (Isaiah 6:1-8)

Does this match your view of God? Have you realised yet that God isn't an ogre but loving without limit and good without remainder? That doesn't mean he doesn't care about evil and sin. God hates our selfishness, not because he's full of hate, but because he's full of goodness and can't tolerate sin forever. But this is why God's love led Jesus to the cross, to deal with sin once and for all. And so God is always love; always good.

God our Father

> So in Christ Jesus you are all children of God through faith, for all of you who were baptized into Christ have clothed yourselves with Christ. There is neither Jew nor Greek, neither slave nor free, neither male nor female, for you are all one in Christ Jesus... Because you are his sons, God sent the Spirit of his Son into our hearts, the Spirit who calls out, *"Abba*, Father."
>
> **Galatians 3:26-27, 4:6**

When Paul wrote this letter, in the 1st Century AD, a son was the most privileged young member of the family. But Paul explains that, whether we're male or female, there's a place for us as 'children of God'. None of us deserve this, but through faith in Christ Jesus and baptism in his name, we receive what only Jesus ever earned - 'the right to become children of God' (John 1:12). Now God's Holy Spirit within us cries out to God 'Abba' (Father). Paul's talking about that deep, intimate longing for God in every Christian which we express whenever we pray to him.

If God is a father, what kind of father is he? Well, he's not necessarily like any dad you've ever had. Look back at the list of God's characteristics:

In what ways has your father been a good picture of God to you?

In what ways has he not?

If your earthly father has mistreated or abandoned you, it will take time to see how different God is. No one was more frustrated with this problem than Jesus. He knew God as 'Abba' - the word in Jesus' native language (Aramaic) for father, or daddy. Jesus couldn't escape the sense of his Father's pleasure and love.

'How great is the love the Father has lavished on us' wrote John, in amazement (1 John 3:1). Until you grasp that love, not just in your mind but in your heart, something deep inside will remain broken and empty. But once you taste the love that God longs to pour into your heart, no substitute identity is ever good enough. To be a child of God is all you need.

No one loves us like God does. As one author wrote, 'there is nothing we can do to make God love us less. There is nothing we can do to make God love us more'. Or put it another way - if God had a wallet, your picture would be in it, and when he took it out it would make him smile.

⌛ Closer to God

Pick one of God's characteristics - the one you find hardest to believe - and look up the Bible verses that go with it.

Try praying to God as 'Abba' or 'Father', your loving, perfect parent. Bring all your concerns to him now, knowing his great care for you, and ask him to show you who he is.

Completely Forgiven

A man was running from the police having killed someone. He arrived at his brother's house, shirt soaked in blood, still carrying the knife. What did the brother do? Without taking time to explain, he took off his shirt and swapped it with the guilty man. He took the knife and sent his brother upstairs to wash. Then the police arrived.

What would you do if you were totally guilty but someone offered to suffer the consequences for you? And what if this wasn't a trick, but a fair exchange? This is precisely the situation we're in as Christians, and it's why the cross is at the heart of our faith.

No Excuses

We don't often think of ourselves as rebels or criminals. But that's what we have been. Rebels dearly loved by God, but rebels all the same. Each one of us has broken God's rules and lived as his enemy. The word sin may sound a bit strong for our actions, but it's the Bible's way of describing every action, big or small, that fall short of God's standards (Romans 3:23). Sin is a serious matter; deadly serious, in fact. To choose God is to choose life; but to reject him is to choose death. Sin results in death, or, as Paul put it 'the wages of sin is death' (Romans 6:23).

The Great Exchange

God is holy and fair. He can't invite rebellious, sinful people to live with him forever unless somehow he deals with their sin. God's solution to this problem took place one spring afternoon on a Palestinian hillside around 30AD. Jesus, God's own Son and the only human who never deserved to die, was crucified as a condemned man.

We've seen that Jesus always felt his father's love. Always, that is, except once. As he suffered and died on that cross, Jesus experienced all the darkness and evil of sin. He took it on himself, even though he didn't deserve one bit of it. He let sin and death do their worst in his body, and just before he died he felt the pain of separation from his loving Father.

> At noon darkness came over the whole land until three in the afternoon. And at three in the afternoon Jesus cried out in a loud voice, *"Eloi, Eloi, lama sabachthani?"* (which means, "My God, my God, why have you forsaken me?") ...With a loud cry, Jesus breathed his last.
> **Mark 15:34-35, 37**

All this, Jesus did for us. We were the guilty ones, living and dying cut off from God, but Jesus came to live with us, to share our pain and to die as one of us.

> Therefore, since we have been justified through faith, we have peace with God through our Lord Jesus Christ, through whom we have gained access by faith into this grace in which we now stand...
> You see, at just the right time, when we were still powerless, Christ died for the ungodly. Very rarely will anyone die for a righteous person, though for a good person someone might possibly dare to die. But God demonstrates his own love for us in this: while we were still sinners, Christ died for us.
> **Romans 5:1-2, 6-8**

One brother might well suffer for another, or someone might die to save a great person. But for God's perfect Son to die for rebellious sinners - that's incredible. And because he has, we have 'peace with God'. This is what it means to be *justified* - to be right with God. Christians still die, but we don't face the hopeless death we deserved or a fair judgement for all our sins. Jesus died that death for us. Instead we can live our lives with God and look forward to being raised from the dead, just as Jesus was.

What stops you believing that Jesus considers you worth dying for?

Living in Forgiveness

Knowing about forgiveness is not the same as living in it. As well as our own broken memories and scarred consciences, the Bible warns us of the activity of the devil. Satan's influence lies behind all the evil in this world, working to 'kill and steal and destroy' all that is good and godly (John 10:10). In particular, he runs a racket of accusation and deception against Christians, plundering their assurance and dredging up their guilt.

What things make you feel condemned?

Consider this verse: 'Therefore, there is now no condemnation for those who are in Christ Jesus' (Romans 8:1).

How much condemnation should we carry round as Christians?

There's an important difference between conviction and condemnation. *Conviction* comes from the Holy Spirit when we sin. It drives us back to God and when we've confessed, owning up to our actions, it is replaced by peace. *Condemnation* is what Satan brings, preying on our insecurities. It hangs around after we've confessed to God and makes us feel unworthy to be a Christian. The best cure for condemnation is to remember the promises of God. Return to the scriptures in this unit, and celebrate forgiveness in the family of God by sharing the bread and wine. Remember, Jesus' blood was poured out for you, 'for the forgiveness of sins' (Matthew 26:28).

You have been forgiven. Now you need to live in that forgiveness. Believe it. Forgive yourself. When you do fall, learn the habit of confessing your sin, trusting God's promises, asking for help and then moving on. 'For as high as the heavens are above the earth, so great is his love for those who fear him; as far as the east is from the west, so far has he removed our transgressions from us' (Psalm 103:11-12).

⧖ Closer to God

Write any sins that you still feel guilty for on a piece of paper. Then confess them and burn or bin the paper.
Read these words from John Newton, the slave trader who, on March 21st 1748 turned to God and found a forgiveness so complete it turned his life upside down.

Amazing grace, how sweet the sound
That saved a wretch like me
I once was lost, but now am found
Was blind but now I see

'Twas grace that taught my heart to fear
And grace my fears relieved
How precious did that grace appear
The hour I first believed

Graciously Included

Imagine telling one of your parents you wish they were dead, running away with your inheritance, wasting the family fortune, disgracing the family name and then returning home bedraggled and desperate.

This is exactly the parable (story) Jesus told to explain how God's grace works. You may know this story well, but the meaning is dynamite.

'Drop dead, Dad!'

Now the tax collectors and sinners were all gathering around to hear Jesus. But the Pharisees and the teachers of the law muttered, "This man welcomes sinners, and eats with them." ...Jesus continued: "There was a man who had two sons. The younger one said to his father, `Father, give me my share of the estate.' So he divided his property between them. Not long after that, the younger son got together all he had, set off for a distant country and there squandered his wealth in wild living. After he had spent everything, there was a severe famine in that whole country, and he began to be in need. So he went and hired himself out to a citizen of that country, who sent him to his fields to feed pigs. He longed to fill his stomach with the pods that the pigs were eating, but no one gave him anything.

"When he came to his senses, he said, `How many of my father's hired men have food to spare, and here I am starving to death! I will set out and go back to my father and say to him: Father, I have sinned against heaven and against you. I am no longer worthy to be called your son; make me like one of your hired servants.' So he got up and went to his father. But while he was still a long way off, his father saw him and was filled with compassion for him; he ran to his son, threw his arms around him and kissed him. The son said to him, `Father, I have sinned against heaven and against you. I am no longer worthy to be called your son.' But the father said to his servants, `Quick! Bring the best robe and put it on him. Put a ring on his finger and sandals on his feet. Bring the fattened calf and kill it. Let's have a feast and celebrate. For this son of mine was dead and is alive again; he was lost and is found.' So they began to celebrate... **Luke 15:1-2, 11-24**

Jesus caused quite a stir by mixing with all sorts, not unlike the way Princess Diana used to visit victims of AIDS or abuse. His outrageous guest list included tax collectors, who had collaborated with the Roman occupying forces, and those labelled 'sinners' by the Pharisees (the religious activists of the day). No wonder eyebrows were raised. But this is what God is like, said Jesus. He's the lovesick Father, scanning the horizon for the first sign of a homecoming. He runs shamelessly to embrace the one who spurned him. There is a place for everyone at his table, Jesus insisted, no matter who they are or what they've done. When anyone turns back to God all heaven rejoices (Luke 15:10)! This is what grace does. It welcomes the sinner, restores the repentant and rejoices over every sign of goodness in this broken world. Grace is the undeserved favour of God. It can't be earned, it can only be given. And God has given it to us. Grace is: God's Riches At Christ's Expense.

Notice in the story that the son offers to work for his father as a slave, but the father won't have any of it. We can fall into the same trap - slaving away for God, trying to be perfect, denying our problems, and racking up 'holiness points'. People who live like this are tough on themselves and tough on others. But God's not interested in the deal. Instead, he longs to throw his arms around us and invite us back to the family.

Graciously Included

✎ Do you ever think like this?

- [ ] I need to work hard for God to love me
- [ ] I hate the way I look
- [ ] I can never forgive myself
- [ ] God must love others more than me
- [ ] I'm too broken for God to use
- [ ] I have nothing of worth to offer

We need to learn to trust God's opinion of us. If he says we're forgiven; we're forgiven. If he says we're his beloved, valuable children; then that's just exactly who we are. Thoughts like the ones above would be really worth discussing with your sponsor.

Struggling with Grace

You may know that Jesus didn't end the parable where we left off. The elder son complains to his father about the welcome his disobedient brother has received, and by the end of the story he still refuses to join the party (see Luke 15:25-32). Why does it end like this? Jesus knew that we need to learn to give grace as well as receive it. We all know people we feel aren't good enough, or don't belong. Or we simply don't like them.

Who do you find it hard to accept?

Why do you think this is?

None of us deserve God's love, but all of us have been offered his grace. In fact, accepting yourself and accepting others are actually two sides of the same coin. So we need to go easy on each other and learn to see people as God sees them. Each person is someone 'for whom Christ died' (Romans 14:15).

Your cell group is the number one place where this truth should come alive. I can think of many people who've found in their cell group an acceptance they couldn't have found elsewhere: recovering drug addicts, convicted criminals, lawyers... Seriously, though, is your cell a picture of the grace of God? Do people discover their true worth there? How can you be part of this?

Grace in Action

During the time of Apartheid in South Africa, there were few better symbols of unity between black and white than Desmond Tutu and Trevor Huddleston. These two men, divided by ethnicity but united in Christ, worked together tirelessly against racism. They believed that every human has been made in the image of God, and that racial boundaries have no place in the family of God: 'there is no Gentile or Jew, circumcised or uncircumcised, barbarian, Scythian, slave or free, but Christ is all, and is in all' (Colossians 3:11). This is grace in action. It makes the church an architectural miracle and a building regulations nightmare: a house without walls.

⌛ Closer to God

Praise God for his grace. Let your imagination take hold of Jesus' picture - heaven rejoicing over your return; the arms of God embracing you...

Pray for anyone you find it hard to accept.

Carefully Restored

Every once in a while, it happens. Abandoned in the dark corner of an attic, left to pick up dust, is a priceless painting unseen for decades. The owners are naturally delighted, but before they book a luxury cruise with the auction proceeds, they'll need to call in the restorers.

Every Christian is like an abandoned masterpiece. God knows the beauty he put in you when he made you, and he knows the wonder of what you can become. But restoration is needed. A lot of his original artistry can't yet be seen. Only over time will the true picture emerge, as each layer of grime is painstakingly scraped away. Sometimes the work will be swift and painfully raw. Mostly it will be gradual and gentle. Finally, though, God will display you as you were meant to be - a beautiful creation, perfectly restored.

Destination: Perfection

It's quite hard to get used to, but somewhat like a pretentious chef, God won't finish with us until he brings us to perfection. Take a look at what he has planned for us:

> And just as we have borne the likeness of the earthly man *[Adam]*, so shall we bear the likeness of the man from heaven *[Jesus]*.
> **1 Corinthians 15:49**
> And we all, who with unveiled faces contemplate the Lord's glory, are being transformed into his image with ever-increasing glory, which comes from the Lord, who is the Spirit.
> **2 Corinthians 3:18**

Humans were originally made like God, and God won't be satisfied until, once again, we bear 'the likeness of the man from heaven'. Now, as we focus on God, he is changing us to be like Jesus, the glorious example of all we were made to be. Being like Jesus doesn't mean no longer being like me, it means learning from his ways and reflecting God to those around us. God isn't looking for an army of clones, but a gallery of masterpieces, each one unique and precious but all telling the same story of grace. If this is God's plan for us then there is hope. As his Spirit goes to work in us, no part of our lives will be left unchanged.

Where in your life do you need hope that you can be transformed?

Out with the Old...

Your destiny as a Christian is to be raised into a glorious new life, just as Jesus was. You'll be finally, wonderfully complete and dwell with God and his people forever in a new creation (see Values 5). But, even now, this process of transformation has already begun. You don't have to change yourself - it's not like starting a new diet or fitness regime - God's power will change you. But you do have a part to play:

> Put to death, therefore, whatever belongs to your earthly nature: sexual immorality, impurity, lust, evil desires and greed, which is idolatry. Because of these, the wrath of God is coming. You used to walk in these ways, in the life you once lived. But now you must rid yourselves of all such things as these: anger, rage, malice, slander, and filthy language from your lips. Do not lie to each other, since you have taken off your old self with its practices and have put on the new self, which is being renewed in knowledge in the image of its Creator.
> **Colossians 3:5-10**

Carefully Restored

Paul isn't saying that changing your behaviour will change your identity. What he says is that you have a new identity - a 'new self'. Because of this, your old behaviour doesn't fit any more. Returning to your old ways would be like changing out of nightclothes into your best outfit, then climbing back into bed. Why do it?

✎ Look over Paul's list. What is still an issue for you?

- [ ] sexual immorality
- [ ] impurity
- [ ] lust
- [ ] evil desires
- [ ] greed
- [ ] anger
- [ ] rage
- [ ] malice
- [ ] slander
- [ ] filthy language
- [ ] lying

Don't be depressed by a list like this. And don't let Satan give you constant guilt trips about these things, but surrender them to God, saying, 'Lord, I know I'm not there yet. Only you can help me. Please deliver me from this struggle in your time and in your way'. In the sections that follow, we'll look at why we get trapped in selfish behaviours and how to change. We'll also look at how to follow God's purpose for us, rather than the destructive ways of our old life.

John Henry Newman once said, 'to grow is to change. To have become perfect is to have changed often'. The Bible says that you *have been* saved (Ephesians 2:5). It also says you *are being* saved (1 Corinthians 1:18) and that you *will be* saved (Philippians 1:28). Salvation is a process, and none of us is yet a finished product. Some of the restoration will happen now, which can include emotional and physical healing, but some will have to wait.

The journey to your destiny will be a long one. On the way you'll face many obstacles. At times, you'll feel like giving the whole thing up. But don't give up on God; he hasn't given up on you.

📖 The Truth About Me

Use these verses to summarise your identity:

I praise God because I have been...
Psalm 139:14

Because of the Father's love, I can be called...
1 John 3:1

I am being...
Colossians 3:10

The one who raised Jesus...
2 Corinthians 4:14

Try saying these words aloud to yourself. You could try to imagine yourself in a safe place with Jesus and hear him say these words to you (this will take time – 20-30 minutes in a quiet place somewhere).

This is your identity, and realising it is the first landmark on the journey. You won't always feel it, but it is still real. It's your greatest treasure; the deepest truth about you. No one can take it from you. Live in it. Let all your actions spring from it. In times of trouble, return to it. It's who you are.

⧗ Closer to God

Look over the Identity material. Ask God to show you what he's been teaching you, and make notes over the page for the Identity meeting.

33

IDENTITY Review

What did you find most helpful in this section?

What did you learn about yourself?

What have you learnt about God?

Is there anything you didn't understand?

What do you need to do?

IDENTITY Meeting

The aim of the Identity meeting is to go over the foundations of the Christian life and to discuss who you are as a Christian.

1. **Do you see some vital signs of faith in your life, and do you feel confident about the fact that you're a Christian? (See Identity 2 and 8)**
2. **Where have you sought identity in the past? What effects has this had? (See Identity 6)**
3. **Which false ideas of God have you ever believed? (See Identity 7 and 9)**

Extra Questions
- Did anything else come up from the review?
- How has the memory verse been helpful?
- Have you set a date for the next meeting (or a fixed time for all 3 meetings)?
- Have you let a group pastor or other leader know you are going through 4Life together?

PRAYER

Pray for anything that has come up from your discussions, or any other important needs you have. Your sponsor can also lay hands on you and ask for you to receive God's Holy Spirit (Acts 9:17). This is especially important if you've just given your life to Christ, or returned to following him. Otherwise they can pray for God to bless you more, 'so that you may know him better' (see Ephesians 1:15-18).

Values

Do not conform to the pattern of this world, but be transformed by the renewing of your mind. Then you will be able to test and approve what God's will is - his good, pleasing and perfect will.

Romans 12:2

We've started with identity, but what comes next? Next we look wider and deeper. Wider into the story of our world; deeper into the priorities that drive you. All the time we have one question in mind: **what's important?**

The bigger picture is essential. If you find your house is built over crumbling mine shafts, you'll do one thing; if you find it's built over a forgotten bank vault, you'll do another. So what is the big picture for our world? Well, it isn't the one dreamed up by politicians, generals and media magnates; it's the one shaped by God. Once you realise his plans for our universe, what's important suddenly changes. This causes us to look inside. Do I value what God values? As with your house, it could lead to tragedy or treasure.

Foundations: Creation

One Autumn day you and a friend step out of your front door and see a trail of evenly-spaced leaves leading down your path and up the road. 'Perhaps someone has laid them out for us'. 'We should follow them and see where they take us'. 'Don't be silly', your friend replies. 'The wind just blew them there. Let's carry on the way we were going'.

There's no knock down proof that God made the world. You won't find God's signature under the pebbles on a beach. There's plenty of evidence, though: the beauty of creation; the way it fits together; and the simple fact that anything exists at all. These things are signs of God's work in our world. He doesn't force people to follow them, but 'God did this so that they would seek him and perhaps reach out for him and find him, though he is not far from any one of us' (Acts 17:27). This is God's world: he created it, shaped it, works in it and has plans for its future.

How you see yourself is important, but so is the way you see the world (your 'worldview'). Creation is the first of 5 vital foundations for a Christian worldview. They're not just ideas to consider or facts to know, they are foundations worth building your life on, and they have a huge effect on our values and actions.

✍ What did you used to believe about the world?

☐ Only humans can save our planet
☐ The world is the product of evil forces
☐ Our future is governed by the stars
☐ God made the world and now sustains it
☐ Nothing exists except what you can experience with your 5 senses
☐ God made the world, but then left it to its own devices
☐ The world is divine
☐ The universe has no meaning at all

How did believing this affect your actions?

Beginnings...

Like a child asking a parent about 'the birds and the bees', we need to listen to God to find out where we came from. The Bible's first book, Genesis (meaning 'beginnings') starts like this:

In the beginning God created the heavens and the earth. Now the earth was formless and empty, darkness was over the surface of the deep, and the Spirit of God was hovering over the waters. And God said, "Let there be light," and there was light. God saw that the light was good, and he separated the light from the darkness. God called the light "day," and the darkness he called "night." And there was evening, and there was morning - the first day...
Then God said, "Let us make human beings in our image, in our likeness, so that they may rule over the fish of the sea and the birds in the sky, over the livestock and all the wild animals, and over all the creatures that move along the ground." ...God blessed them and said to them, "Be fruitful and increase in number; fill the earth and subdue it"
...God saw all that he had made, and it was very good. And there was evening, and there was morning - the sixth day. Thus the heavens and the earth were completed in all their vast array.
Genesis 1:1-5, 26, 28 & 31-2:1

Foundations: Creation

✎ How is creation described?

- [ ] Random and accidental
- [ ] Well ordered
- [ ] Thoughtfully made and blessed
- [ ] Very good

What is the role of humans in creation?

This first chapter of Genesis pictures God forming the world over six days. Like a craftsman, he takes his time, lovingly adding each new part in good order: light and dark; sea, sky and land; plants and animals. Everything God makes is good, and last of all come humans, the crown of creation. We were given the task of ruling creation. This doesn't mean destroying it but caring for it, living off it and being God's representatives on the earth.

The idea of creation in six days may not be intended as a scientific description. The Bible is giving a picture of the fact that God made the universe in his own time and in good order.

Warning: God at Work

It's not common to think of God at work in the world. Like over-sleeping students who never rise to see the bin men, many people just assume that the world 'ticks along by itself'. The Bible teaches something else, though - the God we know through Jesus is active worldwide, 'sustaining all things by his powerful word' (Hebrews 1:3).

What we need is new eyes to see that God is at work in his world and that he hasn't given up on it. This is what Jesus saw so clearly - 'Look at the birds of the air; they do not sow or reap or store away in barns, and yet your heavenly Father feeds them' (Matthew 6:26). This is the God of Jesus: the giver of all good gifts; our wise maker; the rightful ruler of the universe.

To be a Christian is to live in the world knowing that God made it and cares for it. It's to look up and see that 'the heavens declare the glory of God' (Psalm 19:1). In fact, every created thing glorifies God simply by doing what it was made to do. Stars glorify God as they shine, birds as they fly, grass as it grows. You could say the whole universe hums with the praise of God.

A Life of Thankfulness

Though this world is broken and tainted by sin, it is still God's world. That's why Paul wrote, 'for everything God created is good, and nothing is to be rejected if it is received with thanksgiving' and that 'God...richly provides us with everything for our enjoyment' (1 Timothy 4:4, 6:17). So the Christian life is a life of thankfulness. God's good creation is our garden: a place to enjoy, a responsibly to share, and a constant cause of praise.

What can you thank God for in creation?

☒ Closer to God

Spend some time thanking God for all the blessings he has given you, one by one.
Praise him for the glory you can see in his creation.

Foundations: Fall

Every day the newspapers carry stories about the brokenness of our world. Murder, rape, torture, war, political lies, greedy scams, injustice, gossip and prejudice - all witnessed by the silent majority who rarely lift a finger to help. But these daily stories are actually part of one overall story, stretching back to the beginning of humanity: the story of the fall.

Now the snake was more crafty than any of the wild animals the LORD God had made. He said to the woman, "Did God really say, `You must not eat from any tree in the garden'?" The woman said to the snake, "We may eat fruit from the trees in the garden, but God did say, `You must not eat fruit from the tree that is in the middle of the garden, and you must not touch it, or you will die.' " "You will not certainly die," the snake said to the woman. "For God knows that when you eat of it your eyes will be opened, and you will be like God, knowing good and evil."

When the woman saw that the fruit of the tree was good for food and pleasing to the eye, and also desirable for gaining wisdom, she took some and ate it. She also gave some to her husband, who was with her, and he ate it. Then the eyes of both of them were opened, and they realized they were naked; so they sewed fig leaves together and made coverings for themselves...

To the woman he [the LORD] said, "I will make your pains in childbearing very severe; with pain you will give birth to children. Your desire will be for your husband, and he will rule over you." To Adam he said, "Because you listened to your wife and ate from the tree about which I commanded you, `You must not eat of it,' "Cursed is the ground because of you; through painful toil you will eat of it all the days of your life. It will produce thorns and thistles for you, and you will eat the plants of the field. By the sweat of your brow you will eat your food until you return to the ground,

since from it you were taken; for dust you are and to dust you will return."

Genesis 3:1-7, 14-19

This passage reveals a deep truth about our species. The original harmony between humans and their Maker was ruined because we fell from God's good purpose for us. In Genesis, Adam and Eve break trust with God and find themselves in a world of suffering, enmity and death under his judgment. But the same storyline is writ large all around us today. We have rejected God's ways and now the world groans under the weight of our rebellion. This is the state of our planet: beautiful yet broken, created for God's glory but scarred by human evil.

God didn't cause this tragedy - as he saw the extent of our evil 'his heart was deeply troubled' (Genesis 6:6). Sin is our responsibility, and somehow we all share in it. Mysteriously provoked by Satan, we have turned our backs on God. But God is the Source of life, and left on the sidelines he can't give us the gift of life forever. So instead he lets us have what we have chosen - a life without the Giver of Life, and its result, which is death.

What does this idea mean for you? What do you feel when you read it?

A Broken World

This difficult teaching is actually a crucial foundation to have in place. It helps us to face the fact that this is a broken world. Suffering, tragedy and death will always grieve us, but they shouldn't surprise us. Christians aren't called to be glib idealists, but to face a broken world with courage. Our God isn't the cause of all catastrophe, or a silent bystander; he's the one who carried a cross for the world and calls us to share some of the pain.

✐ Do good and evil really exist?

- [ ] If something feels right, it will be
- [ ] Sin, evil and the devil are outdated ideas
- [ ] If you sincerely believe an action is right, it is right
- [ ] No one can say what is wrong for another person
- [ ] All that matters is that no one else is hurt

There's a popular myth that sin is harmless, fun, and a clever concept to sell chocolate bars with. Tragically, nothing could be further from the truth. Sin is a thief. It takes away our purity and our peace. It steals our potential and, worst of all, robs us of our relationship with God. Sin frees no one; it only makes slaves (John 8:34). This is why God judges sin and hates it with a holy passion.

For all these reasons, none of the answers above is true. Sin means living outside God's boundaries, so only God can make the final call about what is right and wrong. While it's not our job to judge others, God has clearly revealed that certain things are wrong, whatever the person doing them believes.

Know Your Enemy

What does the Bible say about the devil? Not enough to satisfy our curiosity, but more than enough to warn us. You need to know that the devil is real and he poses a real danger. He won't be hiding under every stone; but he won't be far away either, if you're dead-set on living for God. 'Be self-controlled and alert. Your enemy the devil prowls around like a roaring lion looking for someone to devour' (1 Peter 5:8). Satan has several tricks: temptation, suffering, doubt, condemnation and lies. He works with the stubborn human heart to offer us every false enticement possible, and to blind unbelievers to Christianity (2 Corinthians 4:4).

✐ What lies can you see around you?

- [ ] Sexual gratification is your right
- [ ] Drink and drugs are keys to happiness
- [ ] There's no such thing as 'truth'
- [ ] Money and prestige make you somebody
- [ ] Nothing supernatural exists
- [ ] Other:

Thankfully, despite his influence, Satan is a defeated foe, grasping and flailing as he reels from the death-blow dealt by the cross of Christ (Hebrews 2:14). Your job isn't to seek and destroy him, but to resist him and stand firm. There's always a way out of temptation (1 Corinthians 10:13), and we have this assurance: 'the one who is in you is greater than the one who is in the world' (1 John 4:4).

⌛ Closer to God

Ask for the grace to see sin as God does, and confess anything that comes to mind.

You may want to try the following prayer, repeatedly, like breathing: 'Jesus Christ, Son of the living God, have mercy on me, a sinner'

Foundations: Israel

Have you ever sat down with a model-making kit and, after half an hour's puzzling, fiddling and frustration, achieved little more than sticking your own fingers together? But then if you can complete the model, you'll have a scaled-down version of something impressive. You'll have created something wonderful that will bring you praise.

God's response to our fallen world hasn't been to wash his hands of it or scrap the whole thing. He decided to create a model, in a fallen world, of what life should look like. He chose one nation to be a picture of what it means to know God. He chose to lavish his grace on them, to rescue and protect them, and to show them who he was. It meant getting his hands dirty, working with rebellious, selfish people in a broken world. At times it would try God's patience to the very limit. But his desire was to create something that would bring him glory by showing the whole world who he was. They would be his people, Israel.

As part of God's family, the story of Israel is your roots and the third great foundation for Christian values. You'll find the beginnings of the story in the Old Testament.

How well do you know the Bible story and its meaning?

- [ ] Not at all
- [ ] Some parts
- [ ] Well
- [ ] Very well

Israel's Milestones*

The Chosen People God chose one man, Abraham (Abram), and promised that...
Genesis 12:2-3

The Exodus Centuries later, God rescued Abraham's descendants from Egypt using Moses, showing that...
Exodus 3:7-8

The Law Moses led God's people through the wilderness where God said...
Exodus 19:4-5

The Promised Land God led them into a new land, promising that...
Joshua 1:3

Kings Eventually, God set up kings in the land of Israel, like David. God said to him...
2 Samuel 7:16

The Exile In the end, though, the kingdom of Israel split in two and God sent prophets, like Amos, to warn them...
Amos 5:27

Return from Exile After some Israelites returned from exile, they waited for...
Jeremiah 31:31

*See the Bible Guide (p. 104) for more details.

What kind of God comes through in the Old Testament story?
Take a few moments to think about this.

Living in the Covenant

The backbone of the Old Testament is God's commitment to his people. At every point he was faithful to them and called them to be faithful in return. This binding relationship of trust was the covenant (meaning agreement or contract). God's side of the bargain was to bless Israel in the Promised Land; Israel's responsibility was to stay true to God.

One blessing of the covenant was to know how to live in a way that pleases God. The best example of this is the Ten Commandments:

> I am the LORD your God, who brought you out of Egypt, out of the land of slavery. You shall have no other gods before me.
> You shall not make for yourself an image in the form of anything...
> You shall not misuse the name of the LORD your God...
> Remember the Sabbath day by keeping it holy...
> Honour your father and your mother...
> You shall not murder.
> You shall not commit adultery.
> You shall not steal.

> You shall not give false testimony against your neighbour.
> You shall not covet your neighbour's house ... or anything that belongs to your neighbour."
> **Exodus 20:2-4, 7-8, 12-17**

If these rules seem a bit negative, take a couple of minutes to imagine what our society would be like if we all kept them...

These laws mark out a good path, and the Israelites were given everything they needed to follow it: prophets to speak God's words, priests to help them worship (often at the Temple in Jerusalem) and kings to lead them. Still, God knew his people would fail him, and he accepted animal sacrifices as a way for them to ask for forgiveness.

None of this is perfect (which is why we call it the old covenant). God planned something better for his people than wars, animal sacrifices, precise regulations, and unequal treatment of women and slaves. And God made no secret of his ambition: a people who wouldn't just avoid the worst extremes of sin but would truly live as a blessing to 'all peoples on earth' (Genesis 12:3).

This is where we come in. We're part of the new covenant, promised by the prophets. Through Jesus, we've been grafted into the new, worldwide family of God and we are bonded to God in a new relationship of trust. And we've been called to finish the story at last, to 'live a life worthy of the Lord and please him in every way' (Colossians 1:10). Through us, the story of Israel continues... What part will you play?

☒ Closer to God
Pray through the Ten Commandments. Ask God to show you any ways you can please him more.

Foundations: Jesus

If you watch any of Alfred Hitchcock's films closely enough, you'll be able to spot something strange. At a certain point in the movie, Hitchcock himself can be seen in the background. If you don't know what to look for, or where to look, you'll probably miss it. But for those with eyes to see, the director has stepped into the frame.

Jesus is the Divine Director's cameo on the stage of human history. In Jesus, God himself has become touchable and knowable, able to be seen by reliable eye witnesses. As his disciple John wrote, 'that which was from the beginning, which we have heard, which we have seen with our eyes, which we have looked at and our hands have touched - this we proclaim...' (1 John 1:1). Jesus is by far the most important foundation of our faith.

Who is Jesus?

Who is Jesus? It's possible to think of him as a Robin Hood figure - just a noble human leader. Or, on the other hand, we can imagine him like Superman - God in disguise, only pretending to be human. But the reality is much more wonderful: Jesus is both fully human and fully divine.

In the past God spoke to our ancestors through the prophets at many times and in various ways, but in these last days he has spoken to us by his Son, whom he appointed heir of all things, and through whom also he made the universe. The Son is the radiance of God's glory and the exact representation of his being, sustaining all things by his powerful word. After he had provided purification for sins, he sat down at the right hand of the Majesty in heaven.

Hebrews 1:1-3

Who is Jesus?

☐ Just a prophet
☐ The exact representation of who God is
☐ A created being
☐ He was involved in creating the universe
☐ He now reigns with God the Father

Jesus was certainly human, like us - he grew and learned, ate and slept. He knew tiredness, anger, surprise and disappointment; he was tempted in every way, he suffered and he died. But Jesus was also greater than any other prophet who has ever lived, and not just a created being like the rest of us. The man Jesus was also God himself. He was, and is, the Father's only true Son. He is the Word of God (God's own self-expression), who was with God in the beginning, but he 'became flesh and made his dwelling among us' (John 1:14).

The Kingdom of God

When Jesus walked on this planet, he bought all God's treasures with him: God's amazing love, his life-giving Spirit, and his unstoppable power. Jesus came to a broken world and grew up as part of a Jewish nation longing for God's deliverance. And when the time was right, he proclaimed his message: 'the kingdom of God has come near' (Mark 1:15).

What is the Kingdom of God? It's what happens when God comes to the earth to save his people and set the world to rights. God's kingdom is when he rules, when things are 'on earth as it is in heaven'. It's when all heaven breaks loose. This is why Jesus began his ministry, his work, by reading these words

Foundations: Jesus

from the prophet Isaiah, 'The Spirit of the Lord is on me, because he has anointed me to preach good news to the poor. He has sent me to proclaim freedom for the prisoners and recovery of sight for the blind, to release the oppressed, to proclaim the year of the Lord's favour' (see Luke 4:18-19). Wherever these things are done in Jesus' name, they are signs that God's kingdom is coming.

✒ What signs of the kingdom have you seen happening in Jesus' name?

- [ ] miracles and healings
- [ ] people released from evil influences
- [ ] the poor being blessed and helped
- [ ] people finding God's forgiveness
- [ ] joyful praise of Jesus
- [ ] lives being changed for good
- [ ] the world's selfish ways being challenged
- [ ] different types of people living in unity
- [ ] more justice and care for the earth
- [ ] a powerful sense of God with us

The kingdom was God's answer to Israel's hopes. It brought the new covenant, complete forgiveness and the Spirit's power to change lives. It also broke every barrier down in God's people: now every believer is like a priest, both sexes have the full rights of God's children, and Gentiles (non-Jews) can join God's family. The work of the kingdom still goes on. It is God's business on earth; to be a Christian is to make it our business, too.

King Jesus

Nothing has ever happened to the world like the life of Jesus. In his ministry, he defeated Satan by living perfectly and overcoming evil. In his death, he de-

feated sin by suffering the cost of forgiving us. In his resurrection, he defeated death and then returned to heaven to rule with the Father. Every enemy of God's work, Jesus has defeated. And right now he reigns until this victory is made complete throughout the whole universe.

What encourages you about what Jesus has done?

The truth about Jesus has been safeguarded for centuries in the Scriptures and in summaries of the Christian worldview like the Apostle's Creed, below.

I believe in God, the Father almighty,
creator of heaven and earth.
I believe in Jesus Christ, his only Son, our Lord,
who was conceived by the Holy Spirit,
born of the Virgin Mary,
suffered under Pontius Pilate,
was crucified, died, and was buried;
he descended to the dead.
On the third day he rose again;
he ascended into heaven,
he is seated at the right hand of the Father,
and he will come to judge the living and the dead.
I believe in the Holy Spirit,
the holy catholic Church,
the communion of saints,
the forgiveness of sins,
the resurrection of the body,
and the life everlasting. Amen.

⌛ Closer to God

Use the words of the creed as an expression of your faith in God. Then thank God for Jesus and for the signs of his kingdom.

Foundations: New Creation

Long before J. K. Rowling finished her series of Harry Potter books, she jotted down some notes and stored them in a folder somewhere very safe. They contained the last chapter of the last book. Exactly how the plot would unfold was still to be decided, and several of the books were still to be written, but the ending was settled, safe and exactly what the author wanted.

The story of our world began with God and it will end with him. He has plans for the whole of his creation and he's promised to bring them to pass. As the saying goes, 'I don't know what the future holds; but I know who holds the future'.

How would you describe the way you feel about the future?

The End

Reading the book of Revelation (the Bible's last book) is like skipping to the last pages of a novel - we see where we're going, even if it's not exactly clear yet how we'll get there. What we find isn't nightmares about alien invasion or environmental disaster; it's a different story. In these visions, God is the clear ruler of the universe. Despite the evil that makes life almost unbearable, God is winding things up in his own way and in his own time. But his plans include the whole of creation. This is the final foundation for Christian values:

Then I saw 'a new heaven and a new earth', for the first heaven and the first earth had passed away, and there was no longer any sea. I saw the Holy City, the new Jerusalem, coming down out of heaven from God, prepared as a bride beautifully dressed for her husband. And I heard a loud voice from the throne saying, 'Look! God's dwelling-place is now among the people, and he will dwell with them. They will be his people, and God himself will be with them and be their God. "He will wipe every tear from their eyes. There will be no more death" or mourning or crying or pain, for the old order of things has passed away.'

Revelation 21:1-4

In what ways will the new creation be different from life today?

Throw away the harps and clouds from your mental picture of the future. God plans something much more exciting and concrete (except probably not made of actual concrete). He's promised to recreate the universe - to free it from all suffering, death and decay. In this new creation, heaven and earth will belong together, God's glory will no longer be veiled and we'll be free to dwell with him forever.

Your present body won't be able to deal with this new reality, so you'll need a resurrection body - like the one Jesus had when he was raised from the dead. This is your destiny: to live in the new creation with God.

This promise of resurrection, though, is only for those who accept God's grace. People who reject the message of Jesus can only expect to face God's judgment and then 'everlasting destruction' (2 Thessalonians 1:9). This is Hell - not Satan's playground, but God's fair verdict on those who insist on paying for their own sins.

Now and Not Yet

The Christian life is a bizarre mix. On the one hand, the future has already begun. We can taste the powers of heaven, and we can confidently expect that God will welcome us into his kingdom. On the other hand, though, we never stop struggling with sin and suffering as long as we're alive. Christianity is a combination of power and pain; sharing Christ's resurrection life, but also carrying a cross; salvation *now*, but also *not yet*.

What's going on? Well, the new creation is coming bit by bit. Every time someone becomes a Christian there's a 'new creation' (2 Corinthians 5:17). But the full new creation is still to come, so in the meantime we 'groan inwardly as we wait' (Romans 8:23). God has given us a taste of what's to come, but like the world itself we have to hold on till the day God's dream is finally accomplished.

Hope-filled Living

Following Jesus is about being 'transformed by the renewing of your mind' (Romans 12:2). Why do our minds need renewing? Because we don't naturally accept the story God gives us in the Bible. And, like houses built on shaky foundations, when our lives aren't based on God's story, things won't work out as they should.

✎ Which stories do you recognize around you?

☐ Heaven is a place for all nice people
☐ God won't hold humans accountable
☐ All religions are equal paths to God
☐ The universe is meaningless
☐ Life is there for what you can take out of it

Think of the effects these stories have on those who live in them. Why care for others in a world with no meaning? Or why follow the message of Jesus if he's just one option among many?

The stories above are incredibly popular in our culture - probably most of us buy into them a bit. But God's story (from creation to new creation) is different. It provides the only firm foundations for a life lived rightly. And it's a story that invites us in, giving us a purpose we were made for and a hope worth holding onto.

If God's new creation really is coming, what difference should it make to you?

This is what it means to live in hope - to let God's story shape your life and colour your dreams. True disciples don't just live for now. They live for the day when they'll stand before their Saviour in wonder, hoping more than anything to hear the words, 'well done, good and faithful servant!' (Matthew 25:21).

⌛ Closer to God

Look over the readings and let God's new creation inspire your imagination.

Then we shall be still and see;
we shall see and we shall love;
we shall love and we shall praise.
Behold what will be, in the end, without end!
For what is our end but to reach that kingdom
which has no end!   *Saint Augustine*

Values

Amongst the ancient ruins of Pompeii, on the west coast of Italy, lie the preserved forms of people who couldn't flee when Mount Vesuvius erupted in AD79. The eerie shapes give away a surprising amount. In one house a woman died on her way out. What could possibly have prevented her from escaping? The answer lies only feet away: a casket of treasure. She had been busy gathering it and she obviously couldn't leave without it.

What we value shapes our lives. Nothing kept that woman from freedom except the things she valued. It's the same for us.

What are values?

Your values are the things that are important to you. They're an unwritten set of priorities that affect your feelings and your actions. For example, if you **value** your appearance you might **feel** embarrassed if there's a rip in your clothes at a party and then **act** by leaving early. This is how it works: our values shape our feelings, which shape our actions. Values run deep. You can *say* you think something is important; you can *want* to act in a certain way. But your values will decide what you actually end up doing. Shereen felt awful about her excessive drinking and gossiping. She *meant* to change, but one of her key values was to be accepted by others. Despite her efforts, her drunken actions were giving her exactly what she really desired: acceptance. Mark wanted to develop his morning prayer life. In *theory* this was important to him, but in

practice it felt impossible. Why? A big value for him was comfort - the kind he got from crashing in front of late night TV and then sleeping in.

As with taking a taxi, unless you deal with what's driving you, you'll never get to your destination. We all have a set of values and it's these things that really drive us. We may have picked them up from parents (either by copying them, or by rebelling against what we've seen). We may have picked them up from our friends, or the surrounding culture. But to make progress in the Christian life we need to bring them into the light and allow God to change them.

Values at War

What was the greatest battle in all history? Waterloo? The D-Day landings? The greatest ever battle actually took place between two figures in a dusty wilderness: one a starving man, the other a demonic ruler. It was a battle of values. Here's a scene from it:

> The devil led him up to a high place and showed him in an instant all the kingdoms of the world. And he said to him, "I will give you all their authority and splendour; it has been given to me, and I can give it to anyone I want to. If you worship me, it will all be yours." Jesus answered, 'It is written: "Worship the Lord your God and serve him only." '
>
> **Luke 4:5-8**

Which two values did Satan offer Jesus?

The devil offered quite a deal: control over others (authority) and recognition (splendour). Probably many of us would have asked him where we had to sign. But Jesus had different values: obedience to God and humility came first throughout his life. The offer didn't fit those values; so he rejected it.

Do not conform to the pattern of this world, but be transformed by the renewing of your mind. Then you will be able to test and approve what God's will is - his good, pleasing and perfect will. **Romans 12:2**

How do we need to change?

Sin and Satan are still very much in business today, skewing people's priorities towards 'the pattern of this world' and promoting the wrong things to number one in people's lives. But Christians have stepped outside the system, because God is renewing our minds. This means a new worldview (the foundations in Values 1-5) and a new set of values.

Without a deep change to our values, willpower alone will often fail us. Even in church, well-established Christians can still be driven by a desperate need for popularity or influence. These powerful values need to be confronted in love and honesty if we're going to grow.

My Values

This next exercise isn't easy, but completing it carefully will reveal a huge amount about what makes you tick. Try to honestly rank each value (don't put what you *think* should be important, but what currently matters most). If you're unsure which values should be high, imagine if you had to choose between them.

Give each value a rank for you from the most important (N° 1) to the least

— Being wealthy

— Having close friends

— Achieving something significant

— Having an exciting life

— Sharing my faith with non-Christians

— Feeling equal with others

— Living without conflict

— Being free to make my own decisions

— Doing God's will at any cost

— Being admired or widely recognised

— Having a close family

— Being powerful and influential

— Loving others, no matter what it takes

— Having fun

— Having a fit or attractive body

— Feeling happy and fulfilled

— Physical/emotional intimacy with others

Any others?

_____

_____

_____

Closer to God

Look over the passage from Romans, then underline your top 5 values on the list. What do you think God might be saying about them?

Values of Jesus: 1

There is a place where useful things, like towels and fountain pens, are useless, and odd things, like lead weights and over-sized shoes are helpful. Where is it? Underwater. The sights and sensations you'll find there are spectacular. But to experience the underwater world, you need know that things are different there - surprisingly different. The kingdom of God is just the same.

Every generation has its dreams. For us it might be the perfect society (if you're politically minded) or the lottery lifestyle (if you're not). In Jesus' day, the dream was the kingdom of God. One way or another, many Jews hoped for a reversal of Israel's fortunes, for some kind of power and prosperity. Jesus, however, thought differently. In fact his teaching was so strange - like learning to breathe underwater - that many people looked at him as if he were dressed in full scuba gear.

Who is Truly Blessed?

'Bless you' we say when someone sneezes. And a great deal of good it does them. To be blessed really means to be happy; fortunate with the fortune that only God can give. But who is truly blessed?

✎ **What kind of people does our society think of as blessed or lucky?**

- ☐ The rich
- ☐ The poor
- ☐ Those who get what they want
- ☐ The strong and brave
- ☐ Celebrities
- ☐ Those who forgive
- ☐ The talented and intelligent
- ☐ The sick and unhealthy

Some of these are the dreams of our day, some were popular in Jesus' time. But whoever's dreams we're talking about, the message he brought is as challenging as you can get:

> Blessed are the poor in spirit,
> for theirs is the kingdom of heaven.
> Blessed are those who mourn,
> for they will be comforted.
> Blessed are the meek,
> for they will inherit the earth.
> Blessed are those who hunger and thirst for righteousness,
> for they will be filled.
> Blessed are the merciful,
> for they will be shown mercy.
> Blessed are the pure in heart,
> for they will see God.
> Blessed are the peacemakers,
> for they will be called children of God.
> Blessed are those who are persecuted because of righteousness,
> for theirs is the kingdom of heaven.
> **Matthew 5:2-10**

How would you describe what Jesus does to the dreams we often have?

"I'll tell you who'll have the kingdom of heaven (the same as the kingdom of God)," says Jesus. " I'll tell you who'll inherit the earth as God's beloved children. It's not who you think, that's who!"

The poor in spirit means those who are in dire straits and desperate for God. Mourners also taste more than their share of life's misery. The meek aren't doormats, but those who humbly get on with serving God. Who else gets blessed? Everyone who's looking for God's right standards (righteousness); the forgiving peacemakers rather than the vengeful warmongers; and those whose heart purity is more important than the approval of others. Finally, there's blessing for anyone who's willing to come last in the great popularity contest of life for the sake of Jesus.

The Great Reversal

This was nothing less than a revolution in what it means to be the people of God. Out goes military strength, proud prosperity and respectable religious rules. In comes total desperation for God, a life of love in action and the willingness to suffer. We're back to values, and this list of blessings (called the beatitudes) is the biggest reversal of values the world has ever seen. There's no prizes for guessing that Jesus was pretty popular with no-hopers and drop-outs. Instead of trying to airbrush them out of the family photo, he gave them pride of place. More than that, Jesus gave them a taste of the kingdom there and then: forgiveness, healings, joy, a new family, and more. God's power was breaking in to bring blessing, and it has done ever since. So don't be scared. Jesus wasn't suggesting a course in sadomasochism for beginners; he was offering the key to life full of God's blessing and help. Good news for the desperate; good news for anyone. Of course, one farmer's answered prayer for rain is the local cricket club's nightmare. The good news of the great reversal is bad news for some. 'Woe to you who are rich', says Jesus in Luke's

version of these blessings, 'for you have already received your comfort' (Luke 6:24). And sure enough, more than one proud hopeful 'walked away sad' because they were wedded to a comfortable lifestyle that wouldn't match the upside-down values of the Master (Mark 10:22).

Living for Jesus' Values

The challenge of the beatitudes is to ask God to change our values to make them more like his. As that happens, our worries about comfort and status will fall away, and we'll start to see that the kingdom begins with those in need, the people written off by life at large. This approach led one young woman, Jackie Pullinger to buy a one way ticket to Hong Kong and work with drug addicts. It led Mother Theresa to the streets of Calcutta to care for the sick and the dying. Where will it lead you?

Which beatitudes challenge your values?

⌛ Closer to God

There's no greater prayer than the prayer of the kingdom: the Lord's Prayer. Many Christians use it daily to request the blessings of the kingdom for themselves and others.

Our Father in heaven
Hallowed be your name
Your kingdom come
Your will be done
On earth as in heaven
Give us today our daily bread
And forgive us our sins
As we forgive those who sin against us
Lead us not into temptation
But deliver us from evil
For the kingdom, the power and the glory are yours.
Now and forever. Amen.

Values of Jesus: 2

People can give the funniest instructions. One blanket had a label, 'not to be used as protection from a tornado'. A packet of nuts had printed on it, 'Instructions - Open packet; eat nuts'. There was also a sign which said nothing except, 'Do not throw stones at this sign'.

Instructions can be foolish or impossible to follow. But they can also be life-saving and profound. Jesus was once asked what was the greatest instruction of all. His answer shows us exactly what God values.

> One of the teachers of the law came and heard them debating. Noticing that Jesus had given them a good answer, he asked him, 'Of all the commandments, which is the most important?'
>
> 'The most important one,' answered Jesus, 'is this: "Hear, O Israel, the Lord our God, the Lord is one. Love the Lord your God with all your heart and with all your soul and with all your mind and with all your strength." The second is this: "Love your neighbour as yourself." There is no commandment greater than these."
>
> **Mark 12:28-31**

There's never been a clearer expression of the values of Jesus than this. In his answer, Jesus puts together two Old Testament passages which talk about one thing: love (you can find the original words in Deuteronomy 6:5 and Leviticus 19:18). Loving God with all that we have comes first. Loving our neighbour, as much as we love ourselves, comes second.

Who is our neighbour? Big question! It's the others around us. But it's also anyone in need, including those who hate us and anyone rejected by society (see Luke 10:25-37). Instead of ignoring or mistreating them, Jesus' instruction is this, 'So in everything, do to others what you would have them do to you' (Matthew 7:12).

In what ways do you show love for God and for others?

What is Love?

So what is love? It sounds like a silly question. You can't turn on a radio without hearing some glossy teen-band warbling about it, or watch TV without a cosmetics ad claiming to give it to you. The problem is, with so much talk of love (especially romantic love), it's easy to be misled. We need to have God's definition of love and not just one that's been made up by the world around us.

✏ What is real love?

- [ ] Hating or changing yourself to please others
- [ ] Valuing people over things
- [ ] Hiding the truth because someone may not like it
- [ ] Accepting someone's heartfelt decision, even if you disagree
- [ ] Giving someone what they want because you want to avoid their disapproval
- [ ] Learning to listen to people, without interrupting or arguing
- [ ] Speaking the truth without any regard for someone's feelings
- [ ] Being willing to be weak or hurt for the sake of others

Values of Jesus 2

- ☐ Needing to control someone
- ☐ Refraining from helping someone if they long to stand on their own two feet

The most loving thing in any situation isn't always simple, but look at every other statement on the list (the odd numbered ones). In each one, true love has been replaced by something else: self-hate, dishonesty, low self-esteem, rudeness and manipulation. Loving God first means we won't always please those around us. Loving others means giving up our attempts to control or use them. But we also need to love others *as ourselves*. And this means refusing to be a doormat or to change ourselves simply to win approval.

Other people are one of God's greatest gifts to us. Each person we meet is unique. As we seek to love them, we learn more about who we are and what love truly is. But this is where we fall down. We struggle with people who are different to us, and so we judge and criticise them. 'They're too loud... too shy... too serious... too immature...', we say. Often what we're trying to do is make others just like us, and if they don't fit the mould, we reject them.

Many times we need to return to the lessons in Identity 9 - God has accepted us and so we don't need to justify ourselves by doing others down. Then we can start to see our neighbour as someone wonderfully and mysteriously different. Our job is not to judge or control them, but simply to love.

Look at the list again. In what ways do you have difficulty in loving others?

Learning to Love

A great myth of our culture is that love is just a feeling, like happiness or boredom. If it's there, it's there; if it's not, there isn't much you can do. Now love certainly has a lot to do with feelings, and there is a feeling we call 'falling in love'. But true love is as much a choice as a feeling. We *choose* to love. We choose to be honest with a friend, or to give regularly to a charity. We choose to give lifts to the elderly or stick by our spouse. And as we make these choices, God's Spirit teaches us how to love and brings our lives closer to the values of his Son.

⧗ Closer to God

Paul wrote the words below about love.

Read them with the word 'love' in the spaces to catch his meaning.

Read them with the name 'Jesus' in the spaces to see what true love is.

Read them with your name in the spaces for a glimpse of what you were made for.

... is patient, ... is kind. ... does not envy, ... does not boast, ... is not proud.

... does not dishonour others, ... is not self-seeking, ... is not easily angered, ... keeps no record of wrongs.

... does not delight in evil but rejoices with the truth.

... always protects, always trusts, always hopes, always perseveres.

1 Corinthians 13:4-7

Values in Action

What would you do if a member of your cell was made redundant? Would you pray for them? Perhaps you'd offer practical help? One small group decided on something more radical. Until the person found new work, the group clubbed together to match their salary. As John wrote, 'let us not love with words...but with actions' (1 John 3:18).

The Great Commission

We've seen the value Jesus put on loving God and our neighbour. As we look at putting values into action, there's one more command of Jesus we need to consider: his final instruction to his disciples.

> Then Jesus came to them and said, 'All authority in heaven and on earth has been given to me. Therefore go and make disciples of all nations, baptizing them in the name of the Father and of the Son and of the Holy Spirit, and teaching them to obey everything I have commanded you. And surely I am with you always, to the very end of the age.'
>
> **Matthew 28:18-20**

The great commission is the final command Jesus gave: to 'go and make disciples'. Along with the greatest commandments, this is the church's task - to make disciples of Jesus Christ from every nation on earth. How does your own story fit with Jesus' words?

Who told you about Jesus? And who taught you, by their words and actions, how to follow him?

How have you followed Jesus' command to go and make disciples?

UP, IN and OUT

How do God's values work in practice? Think of living in 3 dimensions: UP, IN and OUT. Loving God is the UP; loving others in church is the IN; and loving people outside the church is the OUT. These three values are intended to shape our lives more than any others. We can see them in action from Luke's description of the earliest Christian community:

> They devoted themselves to the apostles' teaching and to fellowship, to the breaking of bread and to prayer. Everyone was filled with awe at the many wonders and performed by the apostles. All the believers were together and had everything in common. They sold property and possessions to give to anyone who had need. Every day they continued to meet together in the temple courts. They broke bread in their homes and ate together with glad and sincere hearts, praising God and enjoying the favour of all the people. And the Lord added to their number daily those who were being saved.
>
> **Acts 2:42-47**

In what ways did the believers show love for God?

How did they show love for each other?

How did they show love to those outside the church?

The early Christians were clearly passionate about sharing their faith, but we

Values in Action

should also notice a few things about this task. First of all, saving the world is God's job. We're called to play our part, but it's the Lord who 'added to their number'. Secondly, this job is one we do together, contributing in different ways, and not alone. Lastly, you don't have to reach for a map and plot your course across the globe just yet (like a huge game of Risk). You can start just where you are, with your circle of influence.

My Circle of Influence

Often when people become Christians, some people around them eventually follow. The culture in which the early Christians lived was such that they were able to bring their whole household with them (see Acts 11:14, 16:15, 18:8). These were the people they knew and loved, the people they lived alongside in their house (what the Greeks called an *oikos*).

Each one of us has a circle of influence, like this. We all have people we know well - family, friends, neighbours and colleagues. As these are the people we have most links with, they're the ones whose lives we can influence the most for good. And they're the best place to start when it comes to demonstrating the values of Jesus.

Write the names of the people in your circle of influence who aren't Christians

_____

_____

_____

_____

_____

Love in Action

What does love in action look like? How might we live out God's values of UP, IN and OUT?

Love for God - in every decision, God should come first. This means learning the habit of surrendering to his loving will.

Love in families - respecting our parents and submitting to each other (Ephesians 5:21-6:4). In many families, love is spelt T-I-M-E.

Love in church - loving one another; accepting, honouring and serving one another; carrying one another's burdens; and being devoted to one another (Romans 12:10). This love should come to life in our cell groups.

Love for the lost - taking opportunities to:
- share our lives with others
- meet their needs even when it costs us
- share what Jesus has done for us

Love in our communities - serving the poor and needy in our local area or the wider world.

Love for friends - this includes being faithful to our friends, sharing honestly, always listening, and never holding them too tightly.

All this is a tall order. Like staring up at a huge mountain, or trying to shop for original Christmas presents. But learning to love is what we were made for. All you do is start from where you are and learn step by step.

In which areas do you think you especially need to learn more about love?

⧗ Closer to God

Spend some time praying for your circle of influence. Ask God to bless them and to help you love them.

Changing Values

Which priorities must take second place?
Luke 14:25-27

In October 1947 pilot Chuck Yeager was pushing the Bell X-1 jet faster and faster in his attempt to be the first human to break the sound barrier. The closer he got, though, the more G-Force there was and the more the plane would shake. In fact, after a certain point, the controls would fail altogether.

What else must we give up?
Luke 14:33

Changing our values is like breaking through the sound barrier. The driving forces behind our life have a hidden power, holding us back from the life God calls us to. The approval we long for from our workmates, the intimacy we crave from immoral sex, our fear of conflict, or desperate desire to prove ourselves - these forces cause our lives to shudder as we start to change. Before the barriers are broken, before God takes his rightful place in our lives, we must confront the values we hold most dear. 'What's wrong with you?', others might say; or 'Don't you love me?'; or 'You're taking this too seriously'. Other opposition will come from within. You may find that you're struggling to even *want* to change, and the doubts and problems seem to be getting worse. This is because in your heart of hearts other values still reign over God's values.

The struggle is a sign of hope, though. It shows that your values are shifting and your world is being slowly transformed. Chuck Yeager did break the sound barrier eventually. The risk was worth it. What about you?

How did Paul's values change?
Philippians 3:7-8

Jesus wasn't contradicting the greatest commandments here - we're not to be hateful towards our families. But he knows what our key values often are: loved ones, our own safety, our possessions. If God's will is going to come first in our lives, there will be a conflict with the other values. When it comes down to a choice, it will be *as if* we hate them. This was Paul's experience. Many things in his life had been valuable, but 'compared to...knowing Christ Jesus' he was willing to *consider* them rubbish. Some of the values that drive us are healthy, others aren't so healthy, but none of them deserve the prime place that belongs to God.

Changing My Values

Like a home make-over programme, the Christian life is about letting a designer loose in your most treasured inner rooms. There's a risk (safari-style wall-paper) but also a benefit (the home of your dreams). But no make-over can happen without losing the old furniture and decoration.

Don't underestimate the pain of this process. It means giving up our secret love affair with the many things that take God's place in our lives. It means learning to surrender - to give God the keys to each part of our lives and let him go to work. 'The reason many are still troubled, still seeking, still making little forward progress', wrote A. W. Tozer, 'is because they haven't come to the end of themselves. We're still trying to give orders, and interfering with God's work in us'.

It's also tempting to simply pretend that our values have changed: to tick the right boxes and say that God is N° 1. It's better to be honest, though, and in the end, the pain is worth it. God's ambitious plans for us are way beyond our feeble imagination. As C. S. Lewis once wrote, 'You thought you were going to be made into a decent little cottage, but he is building a palace. He intends to come and live in it himself'.

Return to your values list (Values 6). Look at the high values. Think of examples of how they affect your actions.

What would you like your top values to be?

What will stop you changing your values?

Time to Change

When we were baptised, we died to the values of this world and came alive to God's values. But your baptism needs to be daily renewed in your life. In particular, there will come a time when your decision for Christ will be tested. You will face a battle of values. Another Christian will hurt you deeply, or you'll face unexpected suffering. A seductive temptation will hunt you down, or you'll gradually realise that you're drifting away from God. At that time, your values will be tested to the core. This is why Jesus calls us to make our choice for him now, before the time of testing comes.

Meanwhile, the process of changing values and developing godly habits will take many years. But don't be discouraged. As one writer says, 'to be changed into the person God wants us to be will take a lifetime. But by happy coincidence, that is precisely how much time each one of us has been given'.

⌛ Closer to God

Look over the Values material and make notes over the page for the Values meeting.
Try to commit the memory verse (p. 35) to your mind.

VALUES Review

What did you find most helpful in this section?

What did you learn about yourself?

What have you learnt about God?

Is there anything you didn't understand?

Is there anything you need to do?

VALUES Meeting

The aim of the Values meeting is to go over the basic Christian story and to honestly share the values which shape your life.

1. Do you understand the foundations of the Christian story? (See Values 1-5)
2. What are your key values? Which values would you like to change? (Values 6 & 10)

Extra Questions
- Did anything else come up from the review?
- How has the memory verse been helpful?
- Have you set a date for the next meeting?

PRAYER
Pray for what you've discussed and any important needs you have.
Take time to confess any values which have taken God's place in your life and commit yourself to his way. You can also pray for your circle of influence (Values 9).

3

Lifestyle

But the fruit of the Spirit is love, joy, peace, patience, kindness, goodness, faithfulness, gentleness and self-control

Galatians 5:22-23

There are two kinds of Christian – those who travel as tourists and those who travel as emigrants. Tourists lock up their possessions and travel in search of satisfying experiences. They pop to the airport shop for a cheap phrase book, and hope to survive by a combination of international charades and shouting. Emigrants are different. They sell up totally and set off in search of a new way of life. On the way, they devote themselves to picking up the language and customs of the place they plan to stay. The Lifestyle unit is about being the second kind of Christian.

God has granted us a visa into his kingdom, but his plan isn't for us to sit on our hands and wait for the new creation. He's calling us to begin the journey now, to pick up the customs of the kingdom, and to leave behind everything we can't take with us. This means asking the question, **how should we live?**

Worship

Imagine being locked away in prison for many decades, then suddenly released into the fresh light of the outside world. Or imagine gazing up one night at a supernova exploding in the sky. What would your reaction be? Whatever it is, it would be pretty similar to worship.

Worship is the 'wow' of the heart that's seen God and the 'thank you' of the life that he's saved. Worship is what happens when the people who have been rescued from the dungeons of sin come to the One whose glory is brighter than a thousand stars.

Praise the LORD, my soul;
all my inmost being, praise his holy name.
Praise the LORD, my soul,
and forget not all his benefits--
who forgives all your sins
and heals all your diseases,
who redeems your life from the pit
and crowns you with love and compassion,
who satisfies your desires with good things
so that your youth is renewed like the eagle's.

The LORD works righteousness
and justice for all the oppressed.

He made known his ways to Moses,
his deeds to the people of Israel:
The LORD is compassionate and gracious,
slow to anger, abounding in love.
He will not always accuse,
nor will he harbour his anger forever;
he does not treat us as our sins deserve
or repay us according to our iniquities.
For as high as the heavens are above the earth,
so great is his love for those who fear him;
as far as the east is from the west,
so far has he removed our transgressions from us.

Psalm 103:1-12

What does the Psalm thank God for?

What does it say God is like?

The essence of worship is our response to two things: who God is and what he has done. This is the lifestyle of the kingdom: breathing in God's greatness and breathing out praise.

Made for Worship

Human beings have been made for worship. Just watch weekend car-washers, football fans, and shopaholics and you'll see that we always find something more valuable than ourselves to adore. If it isn't God it will be something, or someone, else. That's the tragedy of a life lived without God - pouring your life's devotion into something that isn't worth it.

But God is worth it. Worship of God is our true purpose. Once we've seen his greatness, worship is as necessary as reaching for a camera in the light of a beautiful sunset.

When we see God, we worship; and when we worship we find that we see God. Worship can be an outdoor pursuit among the wonders of nature or an indoor activity in the quiet of our hearts. But it comes into its own when we gather together in Jesus' name. In the praise of a church or the committed life of a cell group, we put Jesus at the centre of everything we're doing. It's often at these times that his presence with us is most tangible.

Worship

What helps you to worship God?

A Life of Thanks

Worship isn't just an activity; it's a lifestyle. A lavish wedding is no substitute for a lifetime of commitment when it comes to building a marriage. In the same way, our love for God needs to be shown with the whole of our lives.

> Therefore, I urge you, brothers, in view of God's mercy, to offer your bodies as living sacrifices, holy and pleasing to God - this is your spiritual act of worship. **Romans 12:1**

What is God most interested in?

- [ ] Beautiful services dedicated to him
- [ ] Exuberant and skilful praise music
- [ ] Obedient lives, offered back to him
- [ ] Ceaseless activity in his name

Worship can involve many styles of praise and dedication, including the ones listed above, but the heart of worship is the offering of your whole self to God (the third answer). Without obedience, any music we make is just noise (see Isaiah 1:13-17). But service that doesn't spring from a thankful heart is just as useless.

This is why worship comes first in Christian lifestyle. Everything we do in God's name is only worship. We're not trying to justify ourselves (he has done that), we're not trying to save the world (he has promised to do that), we're simply wanting to say 'thank you' to a loving Saviour, whose beauty surpasses all telling. In fact, all the disciplines of Christian lifestyle - whether it's prayer, Bible reading, fellowship or holy living

- are forms of worship. They are the overflow of grateful hearts to God.

The Habit of Praise

Worship often bubbles up naturally. But worship is also a habit we need to develop; and sometimes it's a sacrifice.

Dina made a commitment to God - not to miss any more church services because she wasn't feeling like it. Sure enough, the testing times came, but she stuck by her promise. Over the months, not only did God deepen her faith, but worship began to come more naturally until, in the end, she became a worship leader!

At the end of the day, God seeks worshippers, not consumers. Church services and cell groups don't exist just to satisfy customers; they're for God's glory. Far from being a spiritual filling station for individuals, our gathered worship is part of something bigger. It draws us all together, brings us back to God's great truths, and transforms us bit by bit (sometimes dramatically, sometimes not).

In our prayer life, too, we need the habit of praise. However we may be feeling, God is always worthy of praise. So prayer should often begin with time to worship. In fact, sometimes it's only worship that can lift us out of the gloom and give us the perspective we need.

⧗ Closer to God

Try the ACTS pattern of prayer:

Adoration - praise for who God is and what he has done

Confession - then ask God's forgiveness for sins that come to mind

Thanksgiving - give thanks for every good thing

Supplication - all kinds of requests

Prayer 1

Have you ever tried a new prayer routine? 'This is it', we say to ourselves, 'watch out God, here I come!' 4 minutes and 17 seconds later we've planned our shopping, worried about our day and considered changing the wallpaper. Prayer is difficult. One veteran preacher said trying to keep his thoughts on God in prayer was like walking 17 spaniels at once!

Prayer can be difficult. In the school of prayer there are no short-cuts or comprehensive textbooks. No one can teach you exactly what to say. But then again, no one needs to: prayer is just about you and God, and he himself will teach you all you need to know.

What place does prayer have in your life at the moment?

- [ ] I pray only when I'm desperate
- [ ] I have a set time to pray each day
- [ ] I don't really pray much at all
- [ ] My prayers are mostly like shopping lists of requests for all the people I know
- [ ] I pray for at least 10 minutes most days
- [ ] I talk to God through the day
- [ ] In an average week I'll have several times of deep prayer with God
- [ ] Each day I spend special time with God

Prayer isn't a competition. And, much as we'd like it to, devoted prayer won't earn us Prayer Tokens to trade for the things we'd like. Prayer is relational, not mechanical. Like all relationships it's about talking and listening, growing over time and being changed. Think about it for a second – to communicate deeply and personally with our loving Father. Could there be any greater privilege and joy?

Lessons from the Master

All through his gospel, Luke takes the trouble to let us into the secrets of Jesus' prayer life:

What happened as Jesus prayed at his baptism?
Luke 3:21-22

How did Jesus cope with the great demands of his busy ministry?
Luke 5:15-16

Where and how did Jesus prepare for the crucial choice of 12 disciples?
Luke 6:12

How does Jesus pray as he faces death?
Luke 22:39-44

What did he pray from the cross?
Luke 23:34

Prayer is where Jesus always began. It was through prayer that he knew his identity as God's Son (like at his baptism). Everything he did, especially difficult decisions, sprang from his time with his Father. But prayer was also where Jesus ended up, in every time of trial. It needs to be the same for us. Prayer is the oxygen of the life of faith. It's the place where serving God begins and the fortress we can always run to.

Prayer 1

Honesty

Honesty in prayer is vital. Our prayers can end up as bland as holiday post-cards or as formal as letters to the Inland Revenue. But God is after our hearts. Heartfelt prayer is exactly what we find in the Bible's model prayer book - the Psalms. Here we find 150 prayers of wild praise, red-raw emotion, and stinging questions (see Psalm 55:1-8). Only this kind of honesty can truly bring us close to God.

Prayer is the natural place for every concern the day throws at us. 'Do not be anxious about anything', Paul recommends, 'but in every situation, by prayer and petition, with thanksgiving, present your requests to God. And the peace of God, which transcends all understanding, will guard your hearts and your minds in Christ Jesus' (Philippians 4:6-7).

Prayer is about starting from where you are with the questions you have, the words that spring to mind (or the silence when they don't), and whatever helps you to focus on God. As someone once said, 'Pray as you can, not as you can't'.

What anxieties will you give to God?

☐ Short 'Arrow Prayers', sent up to God throughout the day

☐ Praying in tongues (see Purpose 2)

☐ Praying quietly with open hands

☐ Singing or praying with a worship CD

☐ Using the ACTS pattern (see Lifestyle 1)

☐ Just talking to God as if he was in the room with you

Faith

Prayer starts where we are, but it always leads us to God. This is where faith comes in. As we begin to pray, it can be tempting to say, 'I hope that...' or 'I wish...'. But, while there are no magic words or special formulas in prayer, it's important to pray with faith. Often in the Bible, prayers start with who God is - his power, his love and his plans (see Acts 4:24-31). As we come to God, we remember who he is and that he wants to give us good gifts (Matthew 7:7-11). All this helps us to pray with faith: not wishing but asking, and trusting that God always hears us (there's more on this in Purpose 6).

The disciples asked Jesus, 'teach us to pray' (Luke 11:1). What do you want to learn about prayer?

✍ **Which forms of prayer have you tried?**

☐ Praying set prayers each day (like the Lord's Prayer)

☐ Kneeling or standing to aid concentration

⧗ **Closer to God**

Use the Lord's Prayer (see Values 7), but try praying it bit by bit. After each phrase, pause to reflect on the words and add any prayers that fit. When it comes to 'give us today our daily bread', lay before God anything that worries you.

Prayer 2

As a man was walking through a deserted town centre, a thought popped into his mind. 'Shout 'God loves you!' at the top of your voice'. Feeling pretty crazy, the guy eventually followed the hunch. Nothing happened. Years later he was listening to someone's testimony. 'I was so low at one point that I decided to kill myself', the person said. 'But at that precise moment I heard somebody somewhere shout 'God loves you!'.

Not every Christian has a story as dramatic as that. But every mature Christian has learnt over time to listen to, and obey, the 'still, small voice' which God often gives to guide us.

✎ Have you ever experienced...

☐ a thought that suddenly pops into your mind and seems to be from God
☐ a Bible verse that seems to jump out from the page at you
☐ an impression about someone else which turns out to be helpful and true
☐ A message from a speaker or other Christian that powerfully affects your life
☐ A dream or vision that draws you to God or seems to be from him
☐ an audible voice whose words fit with what God says in Scripture

All the above are ways that God speaks to us. This unit aims to help you hear that voice.

Hearing from God

What is prayer like? It's not as complicated as sending letters to a far away country; but it's not as simple as an average phone call, either. Think of a text message. You send the message and immediately it can be received and understood. But the response you get may vary - you could be called right back, or they might send a message or even turn up at your door. This is more what it's like with God. We know that he hears us, but we can't predict exactly what his response will be.

Christians who are feeling insecure can be desperate to hear from God. We need to remember that God has already spoken clearly to us through Jesus and the message of the Bible (see Hebrews 1:2). God might use all of the ways listed above, but none of it replaces the message of love he has given us in his Son.

A Listening Space

Like a crafty advertiser, God has thousands of ways of getting us to bump into his message as we go through the day. But, as we saw from the life of Jesus, time spent in prayer is crucial when it comes to hearing the voice of God. This is the point of having a listening space. It's a time we set aside to give God our undivided attention and make space for him to speak to us.

> "And when you pray, do not be like the hypocrites, for they love to pray standing in the synagogues and on the street corners to be seen by others. Truly I tell you, they have received their reward in full. But when you pray, go into your room, close the door and pray to your Father, who is unseen. Then your Father, who sees what is done in secret, will reward you."
> **Matthew 6:5-6**

Jesus taught that prayer belongs in a secret place, where we can communicate with our Father God in private. Closing the door includes shutting out everything that distracts us - worries, plans, noises (if possible) and certainly mobile phones! It means stilling your soul. Your listening space could be a set time of your day. You could begin with 10 minutes to pray after reading the Bible each morning. Or it could be something you try to do several times a week, carving out quality time to be with God. A habitual place might be helpful, or a journal to write down what you think God might be saying. What's most important isn't the time or place, but the attitude of your heart - being ready to listen to God.

What has been your experience of listening to God up to this time?

It takes time and practice, but eventually you'll learn to recognise the voice of the Good Shepherd. 'My sheep listen to my voice; I know them, and they follow me' (John 10:27). Sometimes you'll sense that God is saying something. How do we know if these thoughts come from God, from our own minds or from an evil source? Ask yourself:

- Does this fit with the Bible's teaching?
- Is it loving and helpful? (1 Corinthians 14:3)
- Does it fit with other messages from God?
- Do other Christians agree it's from God?

If the thought is right it should pass these tests, especially the first two. In that case, act on it. As you step out in obedience, your hearing will get sharper.

Sometimes, though, you may just share silence with God. 'When you pray, what do you say?' Mother Theresa was once asked. 'I say nothing; I listen', she replied. 'Then what does God say?'

they asked. 'He says nothing; he listens!'

Finding a Pattern of Prayer

How many hours a week do you normally spend on these?

Working	Hobbies
Sleeping	Reading
Eating	TV/Computer
Socialising	Prayer
Family time	Bible reading
Church/Cell	
Other:	

Take a moment to look at the list above. What does it say about your priorities? Before you consider the pattern of your life, it's worth remembering a few things. Firstly, prayer can't just be tacked on to a busy life, like an extra golf lesson. We need to clear space to spend quality time with God by doing some things less. What would you do less?

On the other hand, 'slashing and burning' through your diary like so much rainforest, by rushing too many changes at once, will more than likely burn you out, too! The key is persistence. Some things you may change now; others later. Patterns of prayer work best like water, gradually eroding our hurried, self-centered timetables. It may happen slowly; but it can start now.

Where and when could you find time in your day specifically to pray?

⧖ Closer to God

Don't read any more. Stop now for some listening space. Speak to God from the heart, rest in his presence, and listen...

The Bible

Everyone knows the Bible is an important book, but actually reading it can be pretty difficult at times. It can seem as thick as a phone book, as hard to digest as Shakespeare and as much of a bedtime read as a dictionary.

Why is it so difficult? Partly because the Bible wasn't given to flick through over a two week holiday, but to inspire the people of God for over three millennia. It's also because the Bible is actually a library - a whole collection of books written at different times by different people in different styles. All the pages in your Bible may look the same, but don't let that fool you. Each part is different, and it takes time to get used to its many styles.

Starting Out

As it happens, getting to know the Bible is a bit like feeling your way round a new town. At first, you haven't a clue what's what. Then you'll pick up a feel for the important bits - the main roads, if you like. Over time, you'll develop your own favourite places, and visit some of the lesser known corners. Eventually, if you're willing to make it your home, you'll end up knowing it like the back of your hand. But even then the Bible will constantly surprise you.

So don't worry if the Bible often doesn't make sense. And don't think you have to read it from cover to cover. If you're starting out, begin with a gospel or one of the New Testament letters and read a little at a time (there's also a Bible guide at the back of this book on p. 104).

Don't worry, too, about the tricky bits you find, or let yourself be sucked into pointless arguments. The challenge of the Bible isn't to grasp all the bits you can't understand; it's to obey all the bits you *can* understand.

A Guide for Life

How would you rate each of these as a guide for life (from 1 - 10)?

Internet help
Newspapers
Self-help books
Counselling
Advice from friends
Family traditions
The Bible's teaching
Scientific theories
Your life experience
TV / Films

For the world's best selling book, the Bible isn't all that popular as a guide for life. We're naturally influenced by the other messages around us, and we can get used to turning elsewhere for help with our deepest problems.

But this strange and wonderful text is God's gift to us. The Bible doesn't replace all other forms of knowledge and advice, but it is the key to fitting them together correctly, and by far the most reliable of all. The Bible makes a pretty average bookend, but an unsurpassable guide for life. The only way to test that, though, is to try it out for yourself.

📖 Trusting the Word
What would give Joshua success?
Joshua 1:8

The Bible

What are God's instructions (recorded in the Bible) like?
Psalm 19:7-11

Why was Mary wiser than her sister?
Luke 10:38-42

Where does scripture come from and what it is useful for?
2 Timothy 3:14-17

The Bible is often called the word of God. This is because although humans wrote it, they were 'carried along by the Holy Spirit' (2 Peter 1:21). Their words are human words, full of emotion and honesty, and written from their point of view. But they are also God's words, telling the truth about our world and how to live in it.

How to Read the Bible
The Bible was never meant to be a manual that we store away just in case, or a checklist of beliefs we should agree with. Instead, it's a traveller's guide to the new world of God's kingdom. We need it constantly with us. In fact, we need to be so immersed in its story that the words become part of our bloodstream. How can we do this?

Hear the word - gather together with others to hear the Bible read and explained by those who have studied it. *Share the word* - in your cell God will bring his word to life as you look at it together.

Read the word - find your own personal pattern of reading the Bible, and pray about what you read.

Meditate on the word - this means chewing it over in your mind word by word. You can also let your imagination loose on Bible stories, picturing exactly what it would be like to see them happen or to be one of the characters.

Remember the word - memorising bits of the Bible stores them away so they can encourage you and others when the time is right.

Lastly, and most importantly, we need to *obey the word*. Some older parts of scripture no longer apply to Christians (like Jewish laws about food). Other parts are hard to understand, or seem to clash with what the Bible says elsewhere. But when we know what it says, and receive clear Christian teaching on it, we need to obey. Otherwise we can find blockages in our lives, because we're no longer trusting Jesus as our Lord (see Identity 5). 'Do not merely listen to the word, and so deceive yourselves. Do what it says' (James 1:22).

Which part of the Bible God is calling you to obey at the moment?

⧗ Closer to God
Meditate on the memory verse (p. 57), or pick another verse that's struck you today to memorise. Make some space to listen to God speaking to you through his word.

65

Church

Do you remember the first solo manned mission to the moon? How about the first heart transplant by one surgeon without any nurses or anesthetists? You probably don't. Difficult tasks tend to need teamwork, and Christianity is no exception. Somewhere in history the idea that we can make the journey of faith alone crept into the mindset of many Christians. Wherever we got it from, it wasn't from God.

Far from being just a modern buzzword, the concept of community comes from the very heart of God. The God who *is* love expresses that love first and foremost between the Father, Son and Holy Spirit. As we've been made in God's image, this is exactly what we're called to: the same mutual service and deep love we see in the Trinity. Amazingly, this means that our life in community can replicate the very heart and nature of God.

Look back at the description of the early church in Acts 2:42-47 (see Values 9) and see what this looked like in practice.

We Need Each Other

> ...let us consider how we may spur one another on towards love and good deeds, not giving up meeting together, as some are in the habit of doing, but encouraging one another - and all the more as you see the Day approaching. **Hebrews 10:24-25**

Of course, church can be difficult at times. But where else are we going to find the encouragement to live as Christians as 'the Day' of new creation approaches?

Here's the truth about church: we need each other and, in Christ, we're all joined together anyway! As Paul explains, no Christian is an individual unit saved on their own; 'in Christ we, though many, form one body, and each member belongs to all the others' (Romans 12:5).

Life in the Body

Life in one body, like this, requires humility. For instance, we can't all do the same job. Ears are wonderful things, but if you had 10 of them on the end of your hands playing the piano would be difficult. In the same way, each of us is just one part of the body, and God made the parts to be different. Envy, competition and pointless rows are out of place in the body of Christ. Instead God calls us to be united in our diversity and to concentrate on the needs of others. 'If one part suffers, every part suffers with it; if one part is honoured, every part rejoices with it' (1 Corinthians 12:26).

This is what the New Testament is very concerned about: not the style of our meetings, but the quality of our relationships.

Look at Ephesians 4:25-32. What strikes you about the kind of community life God is looking for?

This quality of life together is a high calling and a big commitment. But isn't the world waiting for exactly this kind of community? As Bill Hybels has said, 'there is nothing like the local church when the local church is working well'. What could be more attractive than a loving group of people who support one another, enjoy each other's God given gifts, and serve the wider world? Groups like this, especially cell groups, are key to our personal growth. They are a school of love, where we learn to lay aside our own agendas and to serve one another.

What contribution can you make to the people in your cell?

Levels of Involvement

Humans relate to each other on many levels. We get involved at a *public* level when we're part of crowds in a town centre or at a large event. We mix at a *social* level with our wider families or at a party. The *personal* level is the handful of people we know well - our friends, families and close colleagues. But there's also the *intimate* level where we share ourselves deeply with one or two others, like a spouse or best friend. Healthy involvement in church means seeking to take part on all four levels.

Where are you involved in church at a public level? (Large gatherings of Christians)

Where are you involved at a social level? (Regular meetings for worship and teaching)

Where are you involved at a personal level? (a cell group for encouragement and prayer)

Where are you involved at an intimate level? (Honest spiritual friendship with a 1 or 2 others)

Being Accountable

The last level of involvement - the intimate level - can be the hardest, but it's not about being told what to do or being controlled in any way. It's about a supportive, confidential friendship which opens you up to God and to each other. This is a risk - it means being vulnerable. But it is our choice as to how open we want to be. Good accountability relationships will develop naturally, growing deeper as trust develops over time. This can be very powerful: as James wrote, 'confess your sins to each other and pray for each other so that you may be healed' (James 5:16).

On a scale of 1-5. How honest are you with your cell group?

1   2   3   4   5

How honest are you with your sponsor?

1   2   3   4   5

Who might be a long term spiritual friend for you?

⧗ Closer to God

Spend some time listening to God. Share with him any struggles you are having with your cell or the wider church.

Openhanded Living

An American on vacation went to see the home of a renowned Spanish writer. He found a very simple dwelling with just books, a bed and a desk. 'Where's your furniture?', said the tourist. 'Where's yours?', replied the writer. 'Mine? I'm only passing through here', said the tourist. The writer answered, 'So am I'.

Openhanded living is about living life as if you're passing through. This is hard for those of us who are used to living with fistfuls of worry and palmfuls of stuff. But God asks us to open our hands. As our fingers gradually unfold, he promises to show us another way: 'cast all your anxiety on him because he cares for you' (1 Peter 5:7). Open hands can also be a blessing to others. 'If anyone is poor among your people...do not be hardhearted or tightfisted toward them. Rather be openhanded and freely lend them whatever they need' (Deuteronomy 15:7-8). God is calling you on an adventure of faith. He wants to teach you to trust him and use you to bring blessings to others. But first you must open your hands.

Worries

One of the marks of tightfisted living is worry. Now, a certain amount of worry is natural ('did I leave the gas on?'), and all of us worry sometimes (Philippians 2:28). But worry can also be a major obstacle in the life of faith.

✒ **What are your worries?**

☐ I worry about clothes/ my appearance

☐ I need to have nice things around me

☐ I have deep fears of death and suffering

☐ I worry about money

☐ The fear of failure often bothers me

☐ I fear being alone or rejected

☐ I am often overwhelmed by worry

☐ Other worries:

Do Not Worry

Jesus pioneered a different way:

"Do not store up for yourselves treasures on earth, where moth and rust destroy, and where thieves break in and steal. But store up for yourselves treasures in heaven, where moth and rust do not destroy, and where thieves do not break in and steal. For where your treasure is, there your heart will be also...

"No one can serve two masters. Either he will hate the one and love the other, or he will be devoted to the one and despise the other. You cannot serve both God and Money.

"Therefore I tell you, do not worry about your life, what you will eat or drink; or about your body, what you will wear. Is not life more important than food, and the body more important than clothes? Look at the birds of the air; they do not sow or reap or store away in barns, and yet your heavenly Father feeds them. Are you not much more valuable than they? Can any one of you by worrying add a single hour to their life?

"And why do you worry about clothes? See how the flowers of the field grow. They do not labour or spin. Yet I tell you that not even Solomon in all his splendour was dressed like one of these. If that is how God clothes the grass of the field, which is here today and tomorrow is thrown into the fire, will he not much more clothe you - you of little faith? So do not worry, saying, `What shall we eat?' or `What shall we drink?' or `What shall we wear?' For the pagans run after all these things, and your heavenly Father knows that you need them. But seek first his kingdom and his righteousness, and all these things will be

Openhanded Living

given to you as well. Therefore do not worry about tomorrow, for tomorrow will worry about itself. Each day has enough trouble of its own" **Matthew 6:19-21, 24-34**

Reread this passage and underline the verses that particularly speak to you.

Can you see the irony? Here we are running after treasure but the things we're chasing either run out, wear out, or lead us away from God. How silly, when God longs to give us lasting treasure. All our worrying won't help us one bit, but he will, and he's promised to care for us if we'll seek his kingdom first.

If we only knew our true identity! Then we wouldn't think that we are what we own (Luke 12:15), or be afraid of God (Luke 19:21), or forget the worth of others (Luke 16:19-21). Instead, we'd know that we're children of a loving Father and our hands would open up as naturally as petals in bloom.

Openhanded Living in Action

First of all, openhanded living is a *heart issue.* When we worry and strive, it's as if we don't trust God. 'Keep your lives free from the love of money and be content with what you have, because God has said, "Never will I leave you; never will I forsake you." ' (Hebrews 13:5).

Secondly, openhanded living is an *integrity issue.* If we're no longer clinging to money and possessions, then why would we want to break laws about tax or stealing?

Third, it's a *giving issue.* God's people have often given a 10th of their income to his work (Malachi 3:10). And Christians, though free from Old Testament rules, may want to be even more gener-

ous (2 Corinthians 9:6-8).

Last of all, it's a *lifestyle issue.* 'If any one of you has material possessions and sees a brother or sister in need but has no pity on them, how can the love of God be in you?' (1 John 3:17). What about Christians in rich western countries? If we're honest, we'll admit that we're trapped in a culture that thinks luxuries are necessities and the only way to enjoy something is to own it. Instead of seeking constant entertainment and the dreams offered by advertisers (often at the cost of high personal debt), we need to consider a change of lifestyle.

What would openhanded living mean for you?

⌛ Closer to God

Look over this Methodist prayer of commitment. If you feel you can, say it with your hands open.

I am no longer my own, but yours
Put me to what you will,
rank me with whom you will.
Put me to doing, put me to suffering.
Let me be employed for you, or laid aside for you.
Let me be full, let me be empty;
let me have all things, let me have nothing.
I freely and gladly yield all things
to your pleasure and disposal.
And now, O glorious and blessed God,
Father, Son and Holy Spirit,
you are mine and I am yours. So be it.
And the covenant which I have made on earth,
let it be ratified in heaven. Amen.

Uprooting Bitterness

No one can say how deep Gordon Wilson's grief was after his daughter died beside him in the rubble left by a bomb at Enniskillen, Northern Ireland in 1987. Incredibly, later that same day his Christian faith enabled him to say these words: "I have no desire for revenge or retaliation... I forgive the bombers and I leave everything to God."

No matter how much sin damages our world, somehow the power of forgiveness is always stronger. When Jesus died on the cross, it was as if a huge tremor rippled through the entire cosmos. At that moment, every chain of guilt and condemnation that bound humankind and kept us from God was shattered by the force. Now the only chains that remain are the chains we choose to stay in.

The Christian life begins with forgiveness, but it's also a lifestyle of forgiveness. Unless we learn this, we can still get sucked into the devil's influence:

> Do not let the sun go down while you are still angry, and do not give the devil a foothold.
> **Ephesians 4:26-27**

Why Forgive?

> Get rid of all bitterness, rage and anger, brawling and slander, along with every form of malice. Be kind and compassionate to one another, forgiving each other, just as in Christ God forgave you.
> **Ephesians 4:31-32**

A business tycoon once owed the bank £100 million pounds for a failed cruise ship venture. As the bailiffs broke through the door of his mansion, he called the bank manager who, miraculously, decided to cancel the debt. The bailiffs were on their way out when they were amazed to see a cruise ship waiter on the floor and heard a voice from the mansion, "... don't come back till you've repaid the whole £1000!" The story ends with the bailiffs back in to the mansion to finish the job. This is basically the parable Jesus told to explain forgiveness (Matthew 18:23-35). To be a Christian is to have the most immense debt cancelled by God. How could we then refuse to forgive others?

> For if you forgive others when they sin against you, your heavenly Father will also forgive you. But if you do not forgive others their sins, your Father will not forgive your sins
> **Matthew 6:14-15**

The following section can be extremely painful for some. If this is you, think about taking it to your sponsor for their help and support as you work through it.

Why should we forgive?

Is there someone you need to ask to forgive you?

Is there anyone you need to forgive?

How to Forgive

We need to deal with unforgiven hurt, before it hardens our hearts. Seek reconciliation. Seek it now.

Uprooting Bitterness

If it is possible, as far as it depends on you, live at peace with everyone **Romans 12:18**

No one ever said this was easy; sometimes everything within us cries out against it. But true Christian forgiveness is the only thing that can break the chains. It means facing up to the full scale of the hurt, but then forgiving from the heart. True forgiveness doesn't depend on an apology. It doesn't keep a record of wrongs, or go on punishing someone, or publicise what they have done. True forgiveness leaves all that with God. Forgiveness can take time. John was devastated by an old friend's actions. When reconciliation didn't happen, he was plagued with angry thoughts. Slowly he tried to offer them to God, forgiving as best he could and asking for the strength (and even the desire) to forgive. Only over the months did the healing balm of forgiveness work its gentle miracle.

When and how can you seek reconciliation with the people named earlier?

Avoiding Bitterness

We live in an age of high expectations, complaints, and compensation claims. How can we avoid cynicism, bitterness and anger?
The first remedy is a thankful heart. Thankfulness neutralizes the acid of cynicism. Instead of complaining; praise. And instead of criticism:

Do not let any unwholesome talk come out of your mouths, but only what is helpful for building others up. **Ephesians 4:29**

The second remedy is to keep short accounts with others:

If a brother or sister sins, go and point out the fault, just between the two of you. If they listens to you, you have won them over. But if they will not listen, take one or two others along, so that 'every matter may be established by the testimony of two or three witnesses.' If they still refuse to listen, tell it to the church; and if they refuse to listen even to the church, treat them as you would a pagan or a tax collector *[see Identity 9]*. **Matthew 18:15-17**

✐ How should we deal with conflict?

☐ Seek the opinion of friends first
☐ Stew on it moodily for months
☐ Deal with it face to face
☐ Have it out in public

Here's a refreshing change to the usual resentment, gossip and cold shoulder approach. Instead, go only to the person concerned and sort it out - option 3 (of course, if it's not serious enough for that, then get over it and keep it to yourself!).
The next step is still done face to face but with others, too, so much better than phone calls, emails or letters.
The last remedy for bitterness is the fruit of the Spirit:

love, joy, peace, patience, kindness, goodness, faithfulness, gentleness and self-control **Galatians 5:22-23**

Each tough situation we face is a challenge. As the tension rises, will we let bitterness do its work? Or will we let the Spirit produce his fruit, instead? If we ask him, he'll calm the storm within us just as Jesus stilled the sea (Mark 4:35-41).

⧗ Closer to God

Listen to God. What is he saying to you about forgiveness?

Dumping Baggage

Have you every had doubts about your luggage as you fly home from holiday? What about that extra bottle of whisky, or the strange ornament that rattles when you shake it? "Anything to declare?" asks the customs officer. . .' People entering the United Kingdom are always asked a vital question "Anything to Declare?" But what about when we enter God's Kingdom?

God . . .

> has rescued us from the dominion of darkness and brought us into the kingdom of the Son he loves'.   **Colossians 1:13**

This is our new location: God's kingdom. But, even though we've been transferred from the kingdom of darkness, we still carry baggage from the time we've spent there - things that don't belong in God's kingdom. God won't throw people out for past mistakes (they've been completely forgiven, see Identity 8), but he does ask us to sort through our luggage and declare anything that needs to be dealt with.

Anything to Declare?

Even though we've been brought into the light, the dark corners of our lives still remain. They're the death throes of our old nature. We each have our own struggles whether its with an addiction, despair, self-loathing, terrifying dreams, uncontrollable anger or simply comforting ourselves by shopping.

As we saw with bitterness, these hindrances can lock us up in a cycle of guilt and they give the devil a 'foothold'. We're still susceptible to Satan's worthless whispers and find ourselves following the old destructive paths we used to take. If we're going to live by the Spirit, it's time we faced up to these things and own up to what's there. Refusing any further links with it we can walk into the glorious freedom God has called us to.

Idols and Influences

You became a Christian when you 'turned to God from idols to serve the living and true God' (1 Thessalonians 1:9). But what is an idol? It's anything that takes the place of 'the living and true God'.

An idol can be quite literally a false religion - the worship of anything other than the God made known in Jesus Christ. But we can also idolize people: our partner, a member of our family, or some other person. When this happens, nothing is more important to us than that person. This is an unhealthy bond. The human soul doesn't flourish in such dry ground - you'll find yourself slowly drawn away from God and others.

We can even make idols of the values that take God's place (see Values 6) and any activities that push God out of the picture. Our culture is falling over itself to offer us God-substitutes: whether it's over-work, a sport, a hobby, or sexual exploits. In each case, something beautiful is twisted out of shape and thrust onto the throne of our hearts where it doesn't belong. Other influences are on offer too, some of which are listed below.

The Hindrances List

It's time to declare your baggage, even past experiences you're no longer involved with.

Dumping Baggage

✎ Which items on this list have you experienced in your life?

☐ Involvement with a cult/ the masons
☐ Involvement in another religion
☐ New age practice: meditation, crystals, etc
☐ The strong influence of horror films/ books, or music that celebrates evil

☐ Addiction to alcohol or smoking
☐ Drug or solvent abuse
☐ Addiction to lust, porn or masturbation
☐ Uncontrollable sexual desires

☐ Strong pride and stubbornness
☐ Extreme bitterness towards someone
☐ Uncontrollable anger or violence
☐ A person or activity that takes the place of God in your life
☐ An obsessive interest or unhealthy, controlling relationship

☐ Extreme depression and suicidal thoughts
☐ Constant feelings of doubt / unworthiness
☐ Overwhelming fear of something
☐ An eating disorder / self-harm

☐ Involvement with the occult, spiritualism, Satanism or witchcraft
☐ Horoscopes or fortune-telling

The reason these items are on the list is that Satan uses all of them to keep us from God and our freedom in Christ. Some you might have had no choice in. Some, like depression, might be closely linked with your personality. Some you still might not feel are unhelpful. Even things done in the distant past need to be faced, and disowned.

Circle the box by anything on the list that's still an issue in your life

Left Luggage

There's no one way to deal with these issues. They are complicated and sensitive, especially when they're linked to an experience of abuse or another trauma. But God wants you to be free:

It is for freedom that Christ has set us free
Galatians 5:1

In some cases, long-term counselling or support will be needed. Talk to your sponsor or church leader if you think this is the case. But an important step towards freedom is to declare them in the following way.

Set aside some time in a quiet place to reflect:

1 Admit each hindrance to God and, if it seems right, to your sponsor;

2 Ask God to help you recognise any negative influence it has had on your life;

3 Reject the hindrances using the prayer below and being specific about each particular area;

4 Avoid any connections that lead you back to the old behaviour (see Lifestyle 10). Where you feel this will be a challenge ask your sponsor to help you by asking you from time to time how you are doing with this.

⧗ Closer to God

A prayer to consider and use:

Heavenly Father,
I praise you for bringing me into the kingdom of your Son and forgiving my sins.
Thank you that you want me to be free.
I confess to you my struggle with............that has kept me from you... (Take time to mention any items on the list)
I now turn away from .... that took your place or stole my freedom in Christ.
Father, cleanse me from the influence this has had and release me from any hold I gave Satan on my life.
I now receive your forgiveness and I choose to live by the Spirit in this part of my life.
In the name of Jesus, who purchased my freedom on the cross. Amen

Pursuing Purity

Imagine an FA Cup-winning football club using the silver trophy to wash their boots in. Or an art gallery storing price-less canvasses on the floor of a box room. It wouldn't happen. When something has great beauty and value, we don't treat it cheaply. Instead, we care for it, protect it, and often make a public show of how valuable it is.

Now think of sex. Try to get beyond the 'sex' that's simulated nightly on TV, or used to sell us toiletries. Think of all that's good about sex:

- It can communicate love
- It can bond a couple together
- It can produce children
- It can be an incredibly intimate way to share yourself and affirm someone else

If, in the right conditions, sex can be this valuable, won't it need some kind of care and protection? What does God think?

God's Plan

Flee from sexual immorality. All other sins a people commit are outside their bodies, but those who sin sexually sin against their own bodies. Do you not know that your bodies are temples of the Holy Spirit, who is in you, whom you have received from God? You are not your own; you were bought at a price. Therefore honour God with your bodies.

1 Corinthians 6:18-20

Why does it matter what we do with our bodies?

Before we look at exactly what sexual immorality is, it's worth asking why God has the standards he has. God isn't against sex, and he doesn't hate our bodies. Instead he's trying to protect our bodies from sin - from being misused, undervalued or put at risk. If we have become God's dwelling place (his 'temple'), and if Jesus paid the price to save us, doesn't God deserve a say in what we do with our bodies?

God's Standards

"Haven't you read," he replied, "that at the beginning the Creator `made them male and female,' and said, `For this reason a man will leave his father and mother and be united to his wife, and the two will become one flesh'? So they are no longer two, but one. Therefore what God has joined together, let no one separate."

Matthew 19:4-6

✎ What is Jesus saying here?

- ☐ Marriage joins a couple as one
- ☐ Marriage is an ideal that God is willing to compromise
- ☐ You can be one flesh with someone without having to think about marriage
- ☐ Marriage is intended for male and female

God has chosen a special place for sexual love – like a trophy cabinet or a picture frame – a place where it can be honoured, kept safe, and enjoyed in all its beauty. That place is marriage. Jesus was very clear that becoming 'one flesh' was something that happened after the public event of leaving parents to live together as man and wife (the first and last answers above).

Why is this teaching necessary? The problem with sex outside marriage is this: it can't promise all that sex is

Pursuing Purity

meant to promise. Within marriage, sex says 'I love you for life'; outside marriage it says 'I love you only for now'. Within marriage it says, 'I love you, only you, and I'm prepared for the consequences of sex'; outside marriage it says, 'I want you physically, but I can't promise anything for the future'. In marriage sex says, 'I fully accept you and I'm willing to back it up publicly'; outside it says, 'I can't make that commitment'. No person's most intimate offering deserves to be treated in that way. Sometimes pressure from our culture or our lack of self-worth makes us settle for that, but it shouldn't.

Purity in Practice

What does this teaching mean in practice? If you're married it means being faithful to your spouse at all costs. It means an end to fantasizing, or flirting with friends and colleagues.

If you're not married it means trusting God for your future. Until God provides the right person for you to marry, you should refrain from all sexual activity. This teaching is hard to follow. It will be especially tough if you feel attracted to people of the same sex. It may also be difficult if you're dating someone who isn't committed to Christ (this is one of the reasons Paul recommends only marrying a Christian - 1 Corinthians 7:39).

Sexual purity is also a mental struggle for many. Chewing over sexual images in your head; seeking them out through TV, magazines or the internet; an addiction to masturbation or fantasizing - all these use in a selfish way the good sexual desires God gave us to share lovingly with one other person.

What can we do? We're surrounded by a culture that prizes sexual expression and individual choice, and we're bombarded with graphic images on a daily basis. But God's loving commands remain. And they are given to keep us from harm and lead us into the best kind of life. He also offers us the power of his grace. God can forgive any sexual sin and give you a new start. Jesus is more than used to dealing with sinners; all he asks is that you reach out your hand and trust him.

Meanwhile, how can we deal with temptation? First of all, remember that it's not actually a sin to be tempted. Even Jesus was tempted. The key is not to *act* on temptation, or wallow in sinful thoughts. As Martin Luther said, 'you can't stop the birds flying over your head, but you can stop them nesting in your hair'.

Remember Paul's encouragement, too, 'God is faithful; he will not let you be tempted beyond what you can bear. But when you are tempted, he will also provide a way out so that you can endure it' (1 Corinthians 10:13).

Is there anything you should talk to your sponsor about?

Closer to God
A prayer to please God in every way:

God be in my head and in my understanding
God be in my eyes and in my looking
God be in my mouth and in my speaking
God be in my heart and in my thinking
God be at my end and in my departing

Breaking Free

How many kids have an imaginary friend at one time or other? It's an obvious way for a child to cope with the experiences of being alone and growing up. But (and I hope this isn't news to you) there comes a time to say goodbye. A time to say, 'I needed you once, but not any more'.

For Christians, too, there comes a time when the habits of our old lifestyle no longer fit. We may have felt we needed them once. But growing up in God means saying goodbye to the pet habits, coping strategies and secret indulgences we once called our friends. God has new habits for us to learn. It's time to break free.

The Struggle

> So I say, live by the Spirit, and you will not gratify the desires of the sinful nature. For the sinful nature desires what is contrary to the Spirit, and the Spirit what is contrary to the sinful nature. They are in conflict with each other, so that you are not to do whatever you want. **Galatians 5:16-17**

The struggle Paul describes here takes place within every Christian. The Spirit is at work in us, growing the character God longs to see - love, joy, peace, patience, kindness, goodness, faithfulness, gentleness and self-control (Galatians 5:22-23). But at the same time 'the sinful nature' (sometimes called the flesh) tries to drag us back into selfish and godless ways.

In the last five units, we've looked at worries, bitterness, all kinds of hindrances, and sexual purity. More than likely, as you've been reading, you've experienced something of the struggle that Paul mentions above.

But don't let this struggle make you forget your identity (this is one of the devil's old tricks). We don't need a godly lifestyle to make us children of God; repentance and faith do that. Instead, a godly lifestyle will grow because we are *already* children of God. Identity comes first. So don't forget the love God has lavished on you and the new start he's given you because of Jesus.

In the meantime, though, the struggle goes on. Don't be discouraged. The fact that there's a struggle at all is a sign that the Spirit is at work in you, challenging sinful desires. Let's not forget the patience of God, either. This is the rock God's people have always returned to: 'you are a forgiving God, gracious and compassionate, slow to anger and abounding in love' (Nehemiah 9:17).

Habit Breaking

Have a look back over recent units.

🖉 **Are there any habits God is calling you to move on from?**
- [ ] Abuse of alcohol or drugs
- [ ] A lazy or fruitless daily routine
- [ ] Gossip or malicious talk
- [ ] Over-work
- [ ] Excessive TV, Internet use or gaming
- [ ] Overspending
- [ ] Impure, hateful or violent thoughts
- [ ] Other:

The following guide (**A**dmit **D**ecide **A**void **R**efocus **T**ry again - ADART) gives practical ideas for tackling lifestyle issues. It's based on the ways

76

Breaking Free

God's people have always used to confront temptation. There's a fuller version at the back of this book (page 106).

Admit

The first stage is often to admit what is going on to God and perhaps another Christian. Face up to the reasons you act in this way (we *always* have reasons for the habits in our lives), confess to God, and ask him to show you any negative influence this behaviour is having on your life.

Decide

The second step is to decide that, with God's help, you're going to tackle the issue. But before you do this, you need to ask: Is this the most important thing I should be dealing with in my life right now? It may not be. God might be more concerned with your prayer life than your thought life; or your anger rather than your smoking.

Avoid

Next, you need to find out what triggers your bad habit. Does it happen most when you're bored, or lonely, or tired? Or perhaps it happens at work or when you're out with friends. Whatever it is, you'll need to change your lifestyle to avoid whatever it is that triggers the problem behaviour. For Graham this meant avoiding getting drunk by setting a two-pint limit down at the pub; for Jez it meant installing an internet filtering programme.

Refocus

Finally, brothers and sisters, whatever is true, whatever is noble, whatever is right, whatever is pure, whatever is lovely, whatever is admirable - if anything is excellent or praiseworthy - think about such things. Whatever you have learned or received or heard from me, or seen in me - put it into practice. And the God of peace will be with you.

Philippians 4:8-9

✎ What is Paul's message?

- [ ] What we see/think doesn't influence us
- [ ] We need to fill our minds with good things
- [ ] Christian habits will bring us peace

Kicking out old habits is never enough; we need to replace them with something. Negative or unhelpful thoughts need to be replaced by good ones. It doesn't take a degree in psychology to work out that filling your mind with the equivalent of junk food - tempting pictures, disturbing messages or hot gossip - will lead to spiritual indigestion. Instead, refocus your thought life on helpful things, and replace old habits with healthy interests and Christian disciplines (see Lifestyle 1-5).

Try Again

You've admitted a problem, decided to change, avoided some of the triggers and refocused your life. But, being human, you may still fail, and need to pick yourself up and try again. This is par for the course of the Christian life. God is teaching you to cling to him, to trust that he's the God of 22nd chances. So take a shower of forgiveness and step back into the struggle. Each small step you are making is a little victory, and for the child of God there are no defeats; only setbacks.

⌛ Closer to God

Look over the Lifestyle material and make notes over the page for the Lifestyle meeting.
Pray through the memory verse and ask for more of the Spirit's fruit in your life.

LIFESTYLE Review

What did you find most helpful in this section?

What did you learn about yourself?

What have you learnt about God?

Is there anything you didn't understand?

Is there anything you need to do?

LIFESTYLE Meeting

The aim of the Lifestyle meeting is to cover the basic habits of the Christian life and confront anything that holds you back as a Christian.

1. **What are your patterns of prayer and Bible reading? How would you like to develop them?** (Lifestyle 2-4)
2. **What hindrances have been at work in your life?** (Lifestyle 6-8)
3. **Where do you feel God is calling you to make changes in your lifestyle?** (Lifestyle 6-10)

Extra Questions
- Did anything else come up from the review?
- Has the memory verse been helpful?
- Have you set a date for the next meeting?

PRAYER

Pray for what you've discussed and any important needs you have. In particular, confess anything that has been holding you back and ask for God's freedom in that area.

Make sure you and your sponsor have time to listen to God together. Ask God if there's anything he wants to encourage you with, and practice sharing and testing the thoughts that come to mind.

Purpose

But seek first his kingdom and his righteousness,
and all these things will be given to you as well
Matthew 6:33

The most wonderful piece of modern art I've seen is a huge blue collage of a person. What's so wonderful? On closer inspection, the whole thing turns out to be made of reclaimed junk. Now God isn't a fan of rubbish - he hates to see good things wasted - but what he does like is reclaiming it. He sought you out and rescued you from a junk lifestyle; he took you in his hands and cleaned you up; now he's making you part of something wonderful. This is your purpose: to be part God's great restoration project - his kingdom.

Don't believe the trendy lifestyle gurus. They'll try to sell you total self-fulfillment in 50 days or less. But God's purpose for us is so much more costly and beautiful than that. It walks the way of Jesus Christ, and it starts when you come to him with the question: **What can I do?**

Filled by the Spirit

I remember my first ever encounter with an electric tooth brush. At first it was as lifeless as your average toothbrush. But one press of a button transformed it into a pulsating whirr of unstoppable dental power! I could barely dare to put it in my mouth. That's the power of electricity.

Like electricity, the Spirit brings things to life. Without his power your faith would be nothing. In fact, without him, there would be no Christian life at all. The unseen Spirit is the power behind God's work in the world. And right now he is at work in you.

📖 Introducing the Spirit

Though he brings power, the Holy Spirit isn't a force; he's a person. He is the third person of the Trinity - God's personal presence in the world. The Spirit is hard to imagine, though, and often described in pictures - as God's breath, a wind or a fire. From the beginning, the Spirit has been with the Father and the Son, like a bond of love between them, and with them he works to redeem creation.

What happened before the earth was formed?
Genesis 1:2

How is the Spirit involved with living creatures?
Psalm 104:29-30

What did God promise his people during their exile from the promised land?
Ezekiel 36:26-27

What did Jesus promise?
John 14:15-17

What happened after Jesus was raised?
Acts 2:1-4

How did Peter know the Spirit could be poured out on Gentiles as well as Jews?
Acts 10:44-46

What must it have been like when the Spirit first came to those followers of Jesus after his death and resurrection? For many centuries, only certain people at certain times had been filled with the Spirit. Now, because of Jesus, all believers can have the experience of being filled with the Spirit. The miracles and experiences Luke records in the Acts of the Apostles are powerful evidence that the Spirit was, and still is, at work in the church.

Seven Works of the Spirit

Trying to define the work of the Spirit is like trying to catch air in your hands (John 3:8). But there are at least seven main ways we can understand how the Holy Spirit works.

Life-giving The Spirit is God's presence in the world (Psalm 139:7) giving life to all things.

Inviting The Spirit is at work as God calls people to become Christians (see Acts 10:1-6)

Inhabiting The Spirit lives in every

Filled by the Spirit

Christian (see Identity 2). He assures us that we are God's children (Galatians 4:6), purifies us from evil (1 Peter 1:2) and marks us out as the people God will save (Ephesians 1:13-14).

Filling The Spirit pours God's love into our hearts (Romans 5:5) as a taste of all that's to come. He also fills us. This can be a fresh blessing for witness and service (Acts 4:31) or an ongoing abundance in a Christian who is open to God (Acts 6:3).

Empowering The Spirit gives various natural and supernatural gifts (see Purpose 2). He also strengthens us (Ephesians 3:16) and helps us to pray (Romans 8:26)

Transforming Over time, the Spirit makes his fruit grow in our lives, giving us Christ-like character (Galatians 5:22-23).

Guiding The Spirit is our guide, convicting us of sin, teaching us the truth, and leading us in the right way to follow God (John 16:8 & 13).

How have you seen the Spirit at work in your life already?

Being Filled

All Christians have been inhabited by the Holy Spirit since the beginning of their faith, but the experience can be very different. For some, it's quite an event (like an inhabiting and a filling together), including a wonderful sense of God's love, and sometimes gifts like tongues or prophecy. For others, it's a quiet occasion when they gave their life to God for the first time.

As we saw above, there's more to the Spirit's work than giving people unusual experiences. However, it's also clear from the New Testament that God wants us to be powerfully filled by his Spirit so that we can know his love intimately and serve him effectively. Some call our first experience of this a baptism in the Spirit, others talk about receiving the Spirit, but the names we use aren't the main issue.

Paul encourages us to keep on being 'filled with the Spirit' (Ephesians 5:18). This means a lifetime of co-operation with the Spirit's work in us. It also means being willing to receive new gifts and experiences from the Spirit, however long we've been a Christian. Tragically we're often held back from this by sin, by doubt, or just by a lack of thirst for God. Are you willing to ask God to show you more of his Spirit's love and power?

How do you feel about receiving more from the Holy Spirit?

scared				peaceful
1	2	3	4	5

Heels dug in			completely open	
1	2	3	4	5

Where in your life would you like to know more of God's Spirit?

⏳ Closer to God

If you then, though you are evil, know how to give good gifts to your children, how much more will your Father in heaven give the Holy Spirit to those who ask him! **Luke 11:13**
Why not open your hands and ask for more of the Spirit's work in your life? You could also ask your sponsor or someone in your cell to lay hands on you and pray for you.

Empowered by the Spirit

What happens when you give children gifts? If they're very little, they might be more interested in the wrapping paper. Older ones might end up using their gift to bash their siblings over the head. But every once in a while, your gift will light up their face and introduce them to a whole world of adventure and fun.

Human nature doesn't really change; it just gets more subtle. The gifts God gives through the Holy Spirit have just the same temptations: confusion, pride and arguments. But like any gift, they have amazing potential, too.

Power to Serve

There are different kinds of gifts, but the same Spirit distributes them. There are different kinds of service, but the same Lord. There are different kinds of working, but in all of them and in everyone it is the same God at work.
Now to each one the manifestation of the Spirit is given for the common good. To one there is given through the Spirit the message of wisdom, to another the message of knowledge by means of the same Spirit, to another faith by the same Spirit, to another gifts of healing by that one Spirit, to another miraculous powers, to another prophecy, to another distinguishing between spirits, to another speaking in different kinds of tongues, and to still another the interpretation of tongues. All these are the work of one and the same Spirit, and he distributes them to each one, just as he determines.

1 Corinthians 12:4-11

Who works through all the gifts?

Why are the gifts given?

Who determines who gets which gifts?

God himself is behind all the gifts: the 'Spirit', the 'Lord' (Jesus) and 'God' (the Father). And it's God who decides which gifts are given, as he works in us 'for the common good'. The gifts of the Spirit aren't exactly talents (like musical ability, creativity, or organisation), though these are of great use for God's kingdom. Gifts come directly from God and rely on him like a kite relies on wind. Some gifts grow over years, others are given instantly. So gifts aren't necessarily a sign of character. This is good news for new Christians, who may find all sorts of gifts at work in their lives pretty soon. But it's bad news for anyone who assumes that a Christian who is greatly gifted is necessarily greatly godly. Unfortunately that's not true.

Gifts Checklist

There are about 20 gifts mentioned in the New Testament, but no one ever set down a definitive list. The checklist below is designed to get you thinking about the gifts God might have given you, or ones he might be leading you to ask for. Spend some time reading the more detailed list of gifts in the Gifts Checklist at the end of this booklet, then use the list with your sponsor when you next meet to see if you can identify your gifts.

✓ ✓ There are lots of signs I have this gift

✓ There are some signs I have this gift

? This is a gift I'd love to have, or think I might have the beginnings of

Empowered by the Spirit

_ I take initiative in starting and looking after new churches (apostleship)

_ I naturally lead Christians (leading)

_ I give good guidance and organisation to projects / groups (administration)

_ I receive encouraging messages from God which strengthen others (prophecy)

_ I explain the Bible clearly to others and pass on Christian truth (teaching)

_ I find many opportunities to share my faith with others (evangelism)

_ I can often tell whether a message is inspired by God (discernment)

_ I receive brief words and pictures from God for other people (messages of wisdom, knowledge and revelation)

_ I can speak in a language of prayer I don't understand (tongues)

_ I sometimes sense a clear meaning behind someone's prayer language (interpretation of tongues)

_ I have seen miraculous answers to my prayers (miracles)

_ I feel a desire to pray for the sick and have seen them healed (healing)

_ I have had an unusual confidence in God, sometimes for unexpected things (faith)

_ I often counsel and care for other people (pastoring)

_ I am passionate about helping strangers, the poor or those who suffer (helping)

_ I can do a particular job to help or care for the needy (serving)

_ I have a strong sense of compassion and forgiveness for others (mercy)

_ I often encourage and support others (encouragement)

_ I feel compelled to give with great generosity to others (contributing to others)

What spiritual gifts do you think you might have?

What other talents and abilities has God given you?

Growing in the Gifts

Spiritual gifts are an unusual phenomenon (in the case of miracles, quite literally). Paul told the Corinthians to 'eagerly desire the greater gifts' (1 Corinthians 12:31) - meaning those which build up the church the most. But Paul also warns against gift envy. God assigns the gifts, not us, and we must avoid the temptation to see them as spiritual promotions or bonuses. Your responsibility is to be faithful with the gifts God has given you, whatever they are.

One place to develop gifts is your cell. Here you can try out your gift in a safe space and benefit from the wisdom and encouragement of others. Who knows, too, what gifts you'll spot or encourage in them?

How could you use your gifts in your cell, church or elsewhere?

⧖ Closer to God

Use your listening space to ask God about your gifts.

If God is giving you a particular gift, make a note above when you've used it to build someone up (if possible, before the Purpose meeting).

83

Serving Others

What do you want to be when you grow up? That's what we ask kids at school, expecting them to say police officer, pop star, train driver or something. But imagine them replying, 'I want to be a servant'.

Being a servant is about as popular today as having flu. We live in a 'me first' culture, and human nature has always preferred glory to service.

✎ **In your everyday life, what do you expect in the work you do?**

☐ I expect thanks for the things I do
☐ Promotion is the mark of success
☐ The bottom line is what matters
☐ Performance will win me respect and status
☐ Motivation comes from financial reward and greater influence
☐ I should make the decisions about things that affect me

Many of these expectations are quite natural when it comes to the average workplace. But serving in the kingdom of God is very different. So different, in fact, that it's much easier for children to grasp than management executives.

The Humble King

Jesus called them together and said, "You know that those who are regarded as rulers of the Gentiles lord it over them, and their high officials exercise authority over them. Not so with you. Instead, whoever wants to become great among you must be your servant, and whoever wants to be first must be slave of all. For even the Son of Man did not come to be served, but to serve, and to give his life as a ransom for many."

Mark 10:42-45

This is where Jesus' topsy-turvy kingdom (see Values 7) began to look absolutely bonkers to the disciples. Its one thing to be generally nice and polite to people, but the top dog should be... well, top dog. Not so, said Jesus. And here he gives a glimpse of something so profound his disciples could barely understand it. In fact they didn't even start to get it until just before he died, when he, the ruler of the universe, knelt down in the dirt to wash their stinking feet (John 13:1-17). I came to be a servant, said Jesus, and that's exactly what you should be too.

It turns out there's something about God - he's not just great and mighty and glorious, but he's also humble. So humble that the clearest view we have of his character is when Jesus Christ, 'being in very nature God... made himself nothing, taking the very nature of a servant' and 'humbled himself by becoming obedient to death - even death on a cross!' (Philippians 2:6-8).

This is a devastating blow to the part of us that thinks like the earlier list. It means that serving others isn't just a bitter pill we have to swallow, or a way of repaying a favour to Jesus, it's actually part of what it means to be like God. That's why the Bible calls us God's children, but also calls us servants.

What is your initial reaction to this teaching of Jesus?

Serving Others

Learning to Serve

✏ **What does it mean to have a servant heart?**

☐ Serving because you are thanked

☐ Serving because it meets your needs

☐ Acting as if your opinions are far better than other people's

☐ Obeying God-given authorities even if it's inconvenient

☐ Paying attention to the needs of others

☐ Being able to give up a role when the time comes

☐ Boasting about your achievements

☐ Speaking lots about yourself and asking little about others

☐ Treating others as if they're less important than you

True servants, who serve from the heart, don't seek to criticise or compare themselves with anyone. They value faithfulness over success. They can serve the Master in the smallest, most thankless task. They're not interested in building their own private kingdoms; the only reward they're looking for is to seek his kingdom first. Rather than fighting their corner, and defending their influence, with John the Baptist they say, 'he must become greater; I must become less' (John 3:30). The first and last 3 answers all fall short of this.

Underline any items on the list above that you struggle with.

Situations Vacant

God cares passionately about the places where you live and work and he's looking for servants who can bring the blessings of his kingdom there. You may feel disqualified for this job. If you do, you're in good company. In fact, feeling disqualified is pretty much a requirement for serving him at all. God has delighted in the flawed service of a whole bunch of misfits, from cynical Sarah to depressive Jeremiah, from washed-up Peter to young Timothy. As Paul explained to the status-mad Corinthians:

'the Lord…said to me, 'my grace is sufficient for you, for my power is made perfect in weakness' …That is why, for Christ's sake I delight in weakness, in insults, in hardships, in persecutions, in difficulties. For when I am weak, then I am strong' **2 Corinthians 12:9-10**

How can you be a servant to those in your cell and your circle of influence?

⧗ Closer to God

Lord, make me an instrument of your peace;
where there is hatred, let me sow love,
where there is injury, let me sow pardon,
where there is doubt, let me sow faith,
where there is despair, let me give hope
where there is darkness, let me give light,
where there is sadness, let me give joy.
O divine master, grant that I may
not try to be comforted but to comfort
not try to be understood but to understand
not try to be loved, but to love.
Because it is in giving that we are received,
it is in forgiving that we are forgiven,
and it is in dying that we are born to eternal life.

A prayer of St *Francis of Assisi*

Witness 1

They say good news travels fast. It could be a tale of breathtaking heroism, the report of a decisive battle, or word of a new miracle cure. News of any one of these would be too good to keep to ourselves, but the Christian message is all three! That's why it's called 'the good news', and why it has spread unstoppably for 2000 years.

Christian witness, or evangelism, means sharing the gospel - the good news about Jesus Christ. Without the witness of a Christian you and I wouldn't have heard the gospel: somebody told somebody who told somebody who told somebody who told us. Now, who will we tell?

What is Witness?

On one occasion, while he was eating with them, he [Jesus] gave them this command: "Do not leave Jerusalem, but wait for the gift my Father promised, which you have heard me speak about. For John baptized with water, but in a few days you will be baptized with the Holy Spirit."

So when they met together, they asked him, "Lord, are you at this time going to restore the kingdom to Israel?"

He said to them: "It is not for you to know the times or dates the Father has set by his own authority. But you will receive power when the Holy Spirit comes on you; and you will be my witnesses in Jerusalem, and in all Judea and Samaria, and to the ends of the earth." After he said this, he was taken up before their very eyes, and a cloud hid him from their sight. They were looking intently up into the sky as he was going, when suddenly two men dressed in white stood beside them. "Men of Galilee," they said, "why do you stand here looking into the sky? This same Jesus, who has been taken from you into heaven, will come back in the same way you have seen him go into heaven." **Acts 1:4-11**

What would happen after the disciples received the Spirit?

Where would the disciples go?

Had Jesus gone forever?

Witness isn't a recruitment drive to put bums on seats in church. It simply means telling others about Jesus. Like witnesses in a court, the disciples' job was just to tell the truth - the truth about who Jesus is and the fact that he's alive and still at work in our world. Starting in Jerusalem, they soon spread out to the rest of Judea. But the message also needed to go to the Samaritans, who many Jews used to despise, and then to reach even to 'the ends of the earth'. All the time they were working to the Master's deadline. One day he will return to claim the world for his own. We have until then to give people the chance to hear the good news (see Matthew 24:14).

Me, a Witness?

Not all Christians have the gift of evangelism (Purpose 2), but all of us are called to be witnesses in some way. This doesn't mean you have to start hurling Bibles at passers-by in the street, or twisting every innocent conversation round to religion ('oh, that sounds like a lovely holiday you've had... but where do you think you're going to spend eternity?'). However, we should look for opportunities to show and to share the good news.

✏ How do you feel about witness?

- ☐ Scared stiff
- ☐ It comes quite naturally to me
- ☐ I feel like I'd be telling people what to believe
- ☐ I'd like to, but don't know how
- ☐ I'm not sure
- ☐ Other:

Why do you feel that way?

Why Witness?

Some of us worry that witness is about changing our personality or changing the facts of our story ('I used to be a drug dealer, then I saw this bright light...' says Harold, the accountant). In reality, though, all it requires is a change of heart.

We've looked at Jesus' command to 'make disciples of all nations' (Matthew 28:19; Values 9). But the preparation he gave for this task wasn't residential courses in marketing, but stories of the outrageous love of God. If only you knew, he would say, how God's heart burns for every wasted life. If you knew how he longs for each rebel to return home, and the lengths to which he'll go to save them from self-destruction. You'd see why I'm doing what I'm doing, and you'd spread the word like hot gossip (Luke 15; Identity 9).

There's no point laying out 'ten reasons to witness'. People who've tasted the extravagance of the Father's love and begun to share his passion for the world have all the reasons they need. As the first disciples said, 'we cannot help speaking about what we have seen and heard' (Acts 4:20). If we believe, too, that Jesus will one day judge all people, then we also know the seriousness of what's on offer.

But the likelihood is that, like me, you may be scared to share your faith. The truth is, we could all do with a heart-change, and not one of us has yet grasped the full extent of God's love. But we do all have one thing: a story. And this is as good a place to start as any.

How would you sum up the good news of Jesus and what he's done for you?

Now ask yourself, is this story worth sharing with others? And am I willing to do this?

God has appointed you as a witness. In due time, he may indeed call you to difficult and godless areas, even to the ends of the earth. But, like the first disciples, he begins by asking you just to start where you are.

⌛ Closer to God

Pray for opportunities to show God's love and share his good news this week. Be careful - God has been known to answer prayers like this!

Witness 2

There are many ways to fish. You can use a rod and bait, or a net. You can even fish with your bare hands. Yes, there's plenty of ways to fish, but not many people fish with dynamite. Another unpopular option is trying to fish without going near the water. It sounds simple, doesn't it? But when it comes to witness, many of us make these mistakes - either blowing non-Christians out of the water, or avoiding them like the plague!

Notice what happed after Matthew the tax collector became a follower of Jesus:

> As Jesus went on from there, he saw a man named Matthew sitting at the tax collector's booth. "Follow me," he told him, and Matthew got up and followed him. While Jesus was having dinner at Matthew's house, many tax collectors and sinners came and ate with him and his disciples. When the Pharisees saw this, they asked his disciples, "Why does your teacher eat with tax collectors and sinners?" On hearing this, Jesus said, "It is not the healthy who need a doctor, but those who are ill. But go and learn what this means: `I desire mercy, not sacrifice.' For I have not come to call the righteous, but sinners." **Matthew 9:9-13**

Instead of ditching his old friends, Matthew seems to have invited them to a party where they could meet Jesus and the other disciples. 'This is just how I like it,' said Jesus to the pious onlookers, 'because I didn't come to rub shoulders with respectable types but to share my message with the people who need it most.'

People become Christians in 1001 different ways, and there are just as many ways you can be involved in the process. But Matthew is a classic example of how it can work. The most natural people for Matthew to introduce to Jesus were his circle of influence, the other tax collectors and 'sinners' (people who broke Jewish purity laws). Rather than searching the streets for people who look as if they're pondering the meaning of life, we should start with the people we already know.

Before we look at an ABCD of how we can witness, make a final note of all the non-Christian friends, family, neighbours and colleagues you know well - your circle of influence (see Values 9).

_____

_____

_____

_____

Ask

Like most things, witness begins with prayer. People can't be argued into the kingdom, or threatened, or enticed with chocolate. The problem is too deep for that: 'The god of this age [the devil] has blinded the minds of unbelievers, so that they cannot see the light of the gospel' (2 Corinthians 4:4).

What is needed is the miracle of faith, and miracles tend to need prayer. This is why Paul says, 'my heart's desire and prayer to God for the Israelites is that they may be saved' (Romans 10:1). Would you be willing to pray daily for opportunities to witness to your circle of influence and ask for their eyes to be opened?

Bless

The second stage of witness is to be a blessing. As the Teacher said, 'let your light shine before others, that they may see your good deeds and glorify your Father in heaven' (Matthew 5:16). When he says this, Jesus is assuming two things. First, he's assuming that we'll be like lights compared to the darkness of this world. This isn't a question of trying to outdo non-Christians, but just seeking to be a blessing wherever we are.

Jesus also assumes that others will be able to see our light. But this won't happen if we're living our lives in vacuum-packed Christian cliques. We need to get out there - out into the places that need light, into our neighbourhoods, into local pubs and clubs, into interest groups and workplaces. Getting out like this will cost time, it may take you out of your comfort zone and into places where it's hard to know how a Christian should behave. But, with the support and prayers of your cell, you can do it.

Can you think of three ways you can go out and be a blessing?

Come and See

How do you evangelize in only three words? How about this - 'come and see' (John 1:46 & 4:29). Witness isn't about shouting answers but provoking questions. When people see the difference Jesus makes to us, they will want to know why. Then we can invite them to find out for themselves. As Peter said, 'always be prepared to give an answer to everyone who asks you to give the reason for the hope that you have. But do this with gentleness and respect' (1 Peter 3:15). As we pray for people and seek to bless them, God will provide opportunities to take things deeper. It could be a conversation about how they see the world, or the spiritual side of life. It could be a chance to share a bit of our story. Or it could mean introducing them to other Christians so they can see Christian community in action and hear more stories of faith. Your job isn't to be a walking encyclopaedia of Christianity but a personal invitation to find out more about Jesus.

Decide

Though some people come to God in a few big leaps, for many others it happens in smaller steps. In the beginning, someone might move from the 'all Christians are weird' place to the 'only some Christians are weird' place. Over time, you might see a change to 'Christians are OK and maybe there's something in it', and so on.

At some point, they will need to decide about the gospel, perhaps after hearing the message several times. And even this isn't the end of the journey but the beginning of the lifetime's work of discipleship! In all this, your job is just to keep praying and keep loving. As she prayed, one woman - Lois - saw her mother move all the way from refusing to even speak about Jesus to taking a step of faith. Are you willing to persevere in love and prayer in the same way?

☒ Closer to God

Pray for your circle of influence. Ask God to take away anything that keeps them from him

Deeper Prayer

May 30th 1999. Alex Ferguson's Manchester United football team are 1-0 down to the mighty Bayern Munich in the closing minutes of the European Champions League Final. Two corner kicks later, the score was 2-1 and United had won. What was the secret of their success? Ferguson's explained after the game, 'You never give in'.

Never give up. That's the secret of success, and it's also the secret of prayer.

> Jesus told his disciples a parable to show them that they should always pray and not give up.
> **Luke18:1**

Sometimes, as Jesus explained, praying to God might feel as pointless as a single mother trying to change European law. But if we don't give up, anything is possible. Now God is no distant bureaucrat, but it does happen to be true that perseverance is one of the deep secrets of prayer. In this unit we press on beyond speaking and listening (Lifestyle 2 & 3) and explore some more of prayer's mysteries.

Intercession

> This is the confidence we have in approaching God: that if we ask anything according to his will, he hears us. And if we know that he hears us - whatever we ask - we know that we have what we asked of him. **1 John 5:14-15**

Intercession is when we stand in the gap between someone else and God to ask for something on their behalf. Whenever we ask or intercede, we should pray with 'confidence'. We're not confident that we have the power to change things (that's why we pray in the first place); our confidence is in Jesus. Because of him we can approach God as beloved children.

How can we show confidence in Jesus? First of all, we ask for things 'in his name'. Jesus said, 'You may ask me for anything in my name, and I will do it' (John 14:14).

Secondly, we need to pray with faith. 'If you believe, you will receive whatever you ask for in prayer' (Matthew 21:22). With this in mind, we need to be specific in prayer: 'Father, give Nina a job before Christmas'. If you pray specifically, God can encourage your faith and bring glory to his name by clearly answering your prayers.

We show confidence in Jesus when we pray with others. God knows what you need before you ask (Matthew 6:8), but praying out loud is a sign of faith in him. It also gives others the chance to exercise faith by agreeing with your prayer, which is why we say 'Amen', meaning 'let it be so'. As with many things, Jesus didn't mean for us to go it alone: 'Again, truly I tell you that if two of you on earth agree about anything you ask for, it will be done for you by my Father in heaven' (Matthew 18:19).

Praying for God's Will

John also mentioned praying 'according to his will'. One of the many insoluble mysteries of prayer is that, while God longs to bless faith-filled prayers, sometimes even our most heartfelt requests will not come about. And so the greatest prayer of all isn't 'give me what I want', but 'thy will be done'. This is the deeper purpose of prayer: not simply to satisfy our wants (James 4:3) but to make us into the kind of people who seek God's kingdom first.

As someone wisely pointed out, God

has five answers to prayer: often 'yes' (1 Kings 20:1-6); sometimes 'no' (Luke 22:42); sometimes 'wait' (Psalm 37:7); or 'mind your own business' when no answer is needed (Acts 1:6-7). Sometimes he even seems to say 'do it yourself', when what is needed isn't prayer but action (Joshua 7:6-10), or when the choice is simply up to us (2 Corinthians 9:7). As we persevere in prayer and seek the wise advice of others, God will make clear to us what his answer is.

Spiritual Warfare

Despite occasionally looking like a harmless hobby, Christianity is serious business. In actual fact, it's a war. Paul explains this in Ephesians 6:10-20, which is worth looking at now. 'For our struggle is not against flesh and blood, but against the rulers, against the authorities, against the powers of this dark world and against the spiritual forces of evil in the heavenly realms' (verse 12).

Our enemies in this world aren't human beings (and they're certainly not other Christians!). Our enemies are the forces of darkness which seek to destroy God's work and keep people bound up in selfishness, lies, and injustice. How can we face such a foe? 'Put on the full armour of God, so that when the day of evil comes, you will be able to stand your ground' (verse 13). Now before you don the celestial equivalent of a chain-mail suit, it might help to notice that spiritual warfare is more practical than it first appears. Our main task is actually just to stay on our feet. Our armour is the truth of our identity in Christ, the lifestyle of righteousness and peace, and the fact that God has saved us (verse 14-17). Hold fast to

this, says Paul, no matter what is thrown at you. But when it does come to attack, God has a weapon for us to use: the message about Jesus Christ (Paul calls it 'the word of God'). As the gospel goes forward more and more people are set free from evil and the forces of darkness are forced to retreat.

This whole spiritual battle, from start to finish, is supported by prayer. We need to be watchful, continually asking to be strong with God's strength, and praying for other Christians as the Spirit helps and guides us (verse 18). We also need to keep praying that the gospel will spread effectively as we and others share it (verses 19-20). This is spiritual warfare.

Going Deeper

✒ Have you tried any of these?

- ☐ Praying out loud in a group
- ☐ Extended times of prayer, even through the night (Acts 12:5 & 12)
- ☐ Fasting: going without food or something else as a sign of serious prayer (Acts 13:2)
- ☐ Interceding for your local area or for world leaders and governments (1 Timothy 2:1-4)
- ☐ Keeping a record of what you've asked for and when requests are answered
- ☐ Keeping a prayer journal (see Lifestyle 3)
- ☐ Receiving prayer to be filled with the Spirit (Acts 9:17-19)

What is God calling you to try?

⧖ Closer to God

Why not plan in time to try one of the forms of prayer above? Ask God to place concerns on your heart that he wants you to intercede for.

Your Work and calling

Do you ever sit down at the breakfast table and, halfway through your cereal, notice a little insignia on the side of the cereal packet that says 'by Appointment to Her Majesty the Queen'? Then you think to yourself, 'wow, I'm not just eating cereal; I'm eating *Royal* cereal. And I didn't even know the Queen liked Sugar Puffs!'

In one way or another, almost all of us work, whether it's studying, a 9-5 job, raising kids, or the tasks of retirement. We can be quite downbeat about our work. But would it alter things if we worked by royal appointment?

Your Work

> Slaves, obey your earthly masters in everything; and do it, not only when their eye is on you and to curry their favour, but with sincerity of heart and reverence for the Lord. Whatever you do, work at it with all your heart, as working for the Lord, not for human masters, since you know that you will receive an inheritance from the Lord as a reward. It is the Lord Christ you are serving. **Colossians 3:22-24**

Paul is writing to slaves here. Though he supported their freedom (1 Corinthians 7:21), Paul knew that slaves often had to live with drudgery and poor conditions or worse. Normally they might be expected to run away, cheat their masters or at least work reluctantly. But Paul's take on slavery, surely one of the worst jobs out there, was this: 'whatever you do, work at it with all your heart'. Why? Because all Christians are working by royal appointment. Your boss may be as sensi-

tive as Attila the Hun and your daily tasks like watching paint dry, but you do have a choice. In your attitude are you 'working for the Lord' - by royal appointment to King Jesus? Are you seeking to bring his kingdom into your workplace?

Our society often encourages us to live for the weekend, or for the money and prestige our work may bring us. But this isn't God's view. In his eyes, every job is worth doing well, whether it's paid or unpaid, noticed or unnoticed, high-flying or low-stooping (in fact, particularly the jobs that serve others). Imagine God had asked you personally to do your work this week. Would you devote yourself to it more cheerfully and wholeheartedly?

✍ **What does your job or daily business allow you to do?**

- ☐ Support myself and my family
- ☐ Help and serve people
- ☐ Share my faith with others (eg. Colleagues)
- ☐ Contribute to human wellbeing
- ☐ Generate money to give to the poor
- ☐ Develop my potential

Hopefully you can see in the list above the many positives that can come from our work. God doesn't just care about Christian meetings and our prayer life; he wants us to do 'something useful' in our work lives. (Ephesians 4:28).

God cares about your work, and he is with you as you work. This is what an 18th Century monk, Brother Lawrence, discovered when he turned the job of endless washing up in a noisy kitchen into an act of praise. 'The time of business', he said, 'does not with me differ from the time of prayer'. Everything he did, however menial, he did as an act of worship to God.

God's Values at Work

Of course, working by royal appointment will make a difference to the way we do our work. For example, imagine if it turned out that Quaker Oats (makers of Sugar Puffs), far from being a respectable purveyor of cereals, were actually rearing baby Sugar Puffs in inhumane factory conditions. That royal insignia would be taken off their packets faster than you can say 'Honey Monster'! In the same way, God wants to give his seal of approval to the work that we do, and also the way we do it.

✎ What are your struggles at work?

- ☐ Temptation to steal/fiddle expenses
- ☐ The lie that wages equal your value
- ☐ Rough treatment from management
- ☐ Unemployment or lack of work
- ☐ Work squeezes out God, family or other vital responsibilities
- ☐ No proper day of rest
- ☐ Bad temper or moodiness
- ☐ Lack of motivation
- ☐ Pressure to succeed/overwork
- ☐ Unjust work practices

Some of the problems above are driven by us: it could be our lack of true identity, or the value we place on achievement (see earlier units). But some issues are not our fault at all. We simply need God's grace and wisdom to cope, and the support of our cell.

Is there anything in you that causes or worsens the struggles you ticked?

How can you be an ambassador for God and his values at work?

God's dream for you

God values any work you're doing now, so long as you can be honest and not exploit others. But he also has a calling for you: something that fits your unique personality, passions, gifts and experience. Fulfilling your purpose is about pursuing God's dream for you. This might be in your current work, in your spare time, or even a different job. But whatever it is, don't be put off by doubts and distractions; 'Take delight in the Lord and he will give you the desires of your heart' (Psalm 37:4).

Catherine's desire was to be a mother, run the marathon and reach young mothers for Christ (not at the same time!). James and Charmian felt called to Pakistan as missionaries. Noreen wanted to be the best Christian head teacher she could be. How about you?

What are some of your dreams?

⧗ Closer to God

Take time to offer your work and your dreams to God with the memory verse in mind.

Justice

A man running a charity stall once tried to sell me a friendship bracelet. 'Let me tell you about the woman who made it', he said. 'If it wasn't for the fair wage she found making these, she would have had to sell her daughter into prostitution'. 'I'll take 3!' I said.

I wish I'd bought more. That's how it is when you feel powerless to do anything to relieve the poverty in the world. You want to do something, but don't know what, and whatever you do seems like a drop in the ocean. At the end of the day, you can still feel guilty about all the things you have that others do without.

But praise God that he came to set us free from guilt. Praise him, too, that he's at work in our hearts to overthrow selfishness, and at work in our world to bring blessing to the poor (Values 7). As we'll see, God cares about justice, but his aim isn't to leave us feeling condemned and useless. God's aim is to inspire us for a purpose: to see this world and its inhabitants looked after in the way he always dreamed. In other words, to see justice on the earth.

📖 God's Heart for Justice

How do God's laws protect the poor?
Exodus 23:10-12

What was planned during a Jubilee year (every 49th year)?
Leviticus 25:39-41

What should God's people be doing?
Isaiah 58:6-7

What 3 things does God require of us?
Micah 6:8

What are the most important matters in Old Testament law?
Matthew 23:23

How did the early church meet each others' needs?
Acts 4:32-35

God knows that in a broken world, sin pulls us like gravity away from his loving ways. So throughout the Bible he calls his people back to justice. He provided for the poor in Old Testament laws, and through the prophets he summoned his people from empty religion to love in action. Jesus shared that same passion for justice, and he challenged the approach that says, 'what's the least I can do without breaking the rules?' Instead, we need the Spirit to change our hearts so we can love each other way beyond what any rules could achieve, which is exactly what we see the early Christians doing.

What forms of poverty and injustice are there in your community?

Putting Things Right

What does it mean to pursue justice? It's all about setting things right. Part of believing in the total goodness of God is accepting that it was never his dream that things turn out like this. He made the world to be beautiful, not ruined; he intended its resources to supply everyone, not just the rich and the powerful. Justice begins when we see the brokenness of our world and take action to set it right. God's values may turn our lives upside down, but when they're unleashed in the world, they actually turn things the right way up - back in line with God's purposes.

Your Part

What part could you play in bringing justice and mercy to the world? William Wilberforce, a talented and promising MP in the 19th Century, devoted his life to the abolition of slavery. Changing society's values was no less painful than the change in an individual, but Wilberforce and other Christian friends persevered. In 1833 slavery was finally outlawed in the British Empire, the year Wilberforce died. He had spent himself on behalf of the poor (Isaiah 58:10).

✐ What action could you take?

- ☐ Support a particular charity or campaign
- ☐ Live on less so you can give money away
- ☐ Get involved locally with needy people
- ☐ Care more for the environment
- ☐ Sell one of your possessions and give the money to the poor

You can't do all the above today (unless you're quick), but God calls us to make a start. You may find God gives you a passion to pray and work for a change in a certain area. This is part of his purpose for your life: each of us has different passions, but all of us can make a difference for God's kingdom.

What areas or issues has God given you a concern for?

⌛ Closer to God

Christ has no body
now on earth but yours,
no hands but yours,
no feet but yours.

Yours are the eyes
through which must look out
Christ's compassion on the world.

Yours are the feet with which
He is to go about doing good.
Yours are the hands with which
He is to bless people now
St Theresa of Avila

Suffering and Waiting

The valley of the shadow of death is no place to be. All colour drains from your world, prayer feels useless, and hope seems an impossibility. You try to close your eyes and focus on God, but when you open them again, life is still cold and barren. Over the days, faith drains out of your heart like water down a plug hole.

You may already know some of the depths of suffering that accompany the life of faith. If not, you'll taste them soon enough. Illness, injury and disability; doubt and depression; hurt and disappointment (even worse when it's caused by Christians); poverty, prison and shame; injustice, grief and death - the servants of Christ aren't exempt from their share of troubles along their way. You might have been sold a life without tears - either a Christianity so comfortable it takes no risks, or an escape from reality. But while Christianity should certainly be powerful, it will also be painful (see Values 5). 'If they persecuted me, they will persecute you also' said the Master (John 15:20). Stark words from a man whose footsteps lead to a cross.

When it all goes Wrong

The Bible is no stranger to sorrow. A cry of grief echoes through its story, from the sufferings of Israel, to the death of Christ and the persecution of his followers. The type of trouble may have changed, but the words of the cry were often the same:

Hear my prayer, LORD;
let my cry for help come to you.
Do not hide your face from me
when I am in distress.
Turn your ear to me;
when I call, answer me quickly.
For my days vanish like smoke;
my bones burn like glowing embers.
My heart is blighted and withered like grass;
I forget to eat my food.
In my distress I groan aloud
and am reduced to skin and bones.
I am like a desert owl,
like an owl among the ruins.
I lie awake; I have become
like a bird alone on a roof.

Psalm 102:1-7

What particular times of suffering or testing in your own life come to mind?

The Bible and Suffering

Why do we suffer? It's a question with many answers, but sometimes none that fit. Suffering is part of living in a fallen world where human selfishness and the forces of evil do their terrible work. That's why suffering will have no part in God's new creation (Values 2 & 5). But is there any purpose to our troubles? The early Christians knew suffering. They often experienced persecution in the Roman world, from social rejection and hostility, to beatings, imprisonment and even death. The New Testament writings address these issues and find several rays of hope. Suffering develops the stamina of our faith: 'whenever you face trials of many kinds...the testing of your faith produces perseverance' (James 1:2-3). Young faith naturally relies on the powerful experiences of the early Christian life. But there are lessons that children can

Suffering and Waiting

only learn outside the safety of the nursery. There comes a time when God calls us to look beyond our feelings and to 'live by faith, not by sight' (2 Corinthians 5:7). At these times we need to cling to God even though he can't be heard or felt or seen, all the way through what's sometimes known as 'the dark night of the soul'.

The Christian who has walked through suffering is stronger - David would never have known the Lord was his shepherd if he hadn't first walked through the valley of the shadow of death and found it to be true (Psalm 23). It is possible, of course, for pain to turn to bitterness. But God's plan is different. He longs to comfort us, and he can use even our sufferings. Your soul may have been gouged deeply by pain, but in time God can use the scars as channels through which love can flow to others. Here's Paul's take on suffering:

> The Spirit himself testifies with our spirit that we are God's children. Now if we are children, then we are heirs - heirs of God and co-heirs with Christ, if indeed we share in his sufferings in order that we may also share in his glory. I consider that our present sufferings are not worth comparing with the glory that will be revealed in us.
>
> **Romans 8:16-18**

What can encourage us in suffering?

For Jesus, the sufferings of the cross came before the glory of his resurrection and ascension to reign with the Father. Paul says here that the pattern will be the same for us. We have the promise of resurrection - 'the glory that will be revealed in us' - and no one can take that away from us. But if we're to share Jesus' destiny, we also need to walk where he walked, sharing God's broken heart for the world he loves - 'we share in his sufferings'.

At the end of the day, though, there's not always a reason for suffering. The book of Job is a sharp warning for anyone who thinks there is. But, like the sun behind clouds, God *is* still there. And he is at work, bringing good out of suffering and weaving the frayed strands of our lives into a tapestry whose beauty will only one day be seen. 'We know that in all things God works for the good of those who love him, who have been called according to his purpose' (Romans 8:28).

Holding On

In the meantime, it helps to be honest with God. Let your tearful questions drive you *towards him* in prayer rather than away from him. And keep on keeping on - one day, one step, even one breath at a time.

> I remember my affliction and my wandering,
> the bitterness and the gall.
> I well remember them,
> and my soul is downcast within me.
> Yet this I call to mind
> and therefore I have hope:
> Because of the LORD's great love we are not consumed,
> for his compassions never fail.
> They are new every morning;
> great is your faithfulness.
> I say to myself, "The LORD is my portion;
> therefore I will wait for him."
>
> **Lamentations 3:19-24**

⧖ Closer to God
Spend time in silence, offering your own struggles to God, or praying for those who suffer now.

What Next?

Congratulations! You stayed the course and finished this stage of the race. Your legs will be stronger now, and your heart healthier. The race goes on, of course, but if you've got this far it's a sign. It shows that the great champion Jesus Christ, who completed the course before us, is pulling you along in his slipstream. And it shows that the multitudes of spiritual athletes who've already finished the race aren't cheering you on in vain (Hebrews 12:1-3).

The Journey So Far

If 4Life was a journey, it wouldn't be a trip to the shops for milk, it would be quite a trek. We began at base camp with things some Christians take for granted (well done for being patient). But by the time we'd covered some of the more challenging foothills, you may not have been able to take in all the views. Below there's a chance to make a note of areas you could go over again, either by returning to the unit or with further reading and prayer. There are also many lofty peaks we've barely glimpsed; even a lifetime wouldn't allow us to scale them all. But what *have* we covered?

1 Identity: This began with new life in Christ. It was also about being plugged into a family of Christians and being willing to grow. This was a time to replace false images of you and of God with true ones.

2 Values: We set out the history of the world, from creation to new creation. Our calling is to live as part of this story, which means changing our priorities. This was a time of challenge: what values are driving you?

3 Lifestyle: Out with old habits; in with new ones. This was a time to develop disciplines like prayer and bible reading. It was also a time to clear out a whole load of old junk, from bitterness to sexual immorality.

4 Purpose: This is about having a vision for your life and the power and perspective to see it through. It's been a time to find your gifts and calling, and also to discover ways to serve God's kingdom around the world.

Return to the vital signs list (Identity 2)

Can you see any new signs, or more of these things in your life?

What have you got out of doing 4Life?

What areas of your life still need to change?

What Next?

Now you've completed 4Life, you may want to continue meeting regularly with someone. Why not also talk to your cell leader about becoming a sponsor (see the Sponsor's Guide, p. 102). You'll probably learn just as much again if you're helping someone else through the experience. As the Openhanded One said, 'it is more blessed to give than to receive' (Acts 20:35).

Your Life's Mission

Now your journey goes on from here. One final aid on that journey might be to come up with a mission statement which sums up your calling and passion in life. Jesus said, 'I must preach the good news of the kingdom of God...because that is why I was sent' (Luke 4:43). But what is your mission?

If you can, make it a memorable and inspiring sentence. Then when the treadmill of life threatens to pull you in, you can remind yourself of the dreams God has placed within you. There should be ideas for you to use if you look back at your dreams (Purpose 7) and the values you'd like to have (Values 10).

What could be your mission statement for your life?

Looking to the Horizon

I once saw a game of poker played with imaginary money. 'Brilliant!', you might think, 'Nothing to lose'. But in fact it was the most boring card game I've ever seen (and that's saying something). Why was it boring? Because there was nothing at stake. Show me the Christian who's bored and I'll bet that 9 times out of 10 they're not really risking much on their faith.

In God's plans for the world, though, there is plenty at stake. Lives are being lived and lost without God; billions have never seen the message of Jesus lived out; the needy, the broken, the desperate - they're all waiting for a sign that God's love is in action on this planet. Are you willing to place your stake on the purposes of God, or are you worried about losing what you have? This is what Jesus meant when he said, 'seek first his kingdom and his righteousness, and all these things will be given to you as well' (Matthew 6:33).

In 1952, one young man, Jim Elliott, put this into action by travelling as a missionary to a tribe in Ecuador. The tribe killed him and four others; his young wife and team were devastated. But no death in the service of the kingdom is ever the final word. One of many blessings to come from his death was that the tribe were eventually reached by Elliot's widow, Elizabeth. Amazingly, before he died, Elliott had written these words: 'he is no fool who gives what he cannot keep, to gain what he cannot lose'.

⌛ Closer to God

Look over the Purpose material, including the memory verse, and make notes over the page for the Purpose meeting.

PURPOSE Review

What did you find most helpful in this section?

What did you find learn about yourself?

What have you learnt about God?

Is there anything you didn't understand?

Is there anything you need to do?

PURPOSE Meeting

The Purpose meeting is about discovering God's gifts and calling for your life, and to looking back at all that has happened through doing 4Life.

1. **What gifts might God have given you? What does your sponsor think**
   (Purpose 2)
2. **What has changed while you've done 4Life? What still needs to change?**
   (Purpose 10)
3. **Where is God calling you in the future?** (Purpose 7)

Extra Questions
- How has the listening space gone?
- Who has God put in your circle of influence? (Purpose 4 & 5)
- Will you let a leader know you've done 4Life and pass on information about your gifts and calling?

PRAYER

Pray for growth in the gifts and calling God has given you, and for any gifts you would like.

You might end by asking your sponsor to lay hands on you and commission you with a prayer like this:

Father God, commission your servant (name). Fill him/her with your Spirit in the name of Jesus Christ. Seal in him/her all you have been teaching, and use his/her gifts in the service of your kingdom. Amen

Sponsor's guide
Bible Guide
Habit Breaking
Gifts Checklist

EXTRA

Sponsor's Guide

So, you've worked through 4Life yourself. How about sharing the experience with someone else? If it fits with the way your church works, you could offer to go through 4Life with someone. 'I wouldn't be able to do it' might be your natural reaction. But that isn't how you got to page 102 of a book like this (unless you're flicking through the pages!). When the time is right, you can do it.

Sponsoring someone through 4Life is a privilege. You'll benefit once again from the Bible teaching that's covered. You'll also form what could be a very precious relationship with another believer. The guidelines below will help with this. It's important, too, that doing 4Life with someone is discussed *beforehand* with your cell leader, so they know what's going on.

Some Practical Stuff

What's basically involved in being a 4Life sponsor?

- Complete 4Life for yourself, unless you are working through it together
- Be wise in forming a sponsoring relationship. Meet with someone of the same gender to avoid problems that could arise from the many personal things you'll be sharing.
- Make time for the meetings. If possible, you might want to arrange a time to chat and pray even before the big 4 meetings, especially if you don't already know the sponsee.
- Each meeting is designed to take about an hour. You may find you both want to meet for longer, but take care that the meetings remain *manageable*. If your sponsee knows that the meeting will only last an hour, they'll feel more confident about coming along.
- In the meeting itself, your job is to keep a reasonable pace and not get sidetracked. Concentrate on the 2-3 main questions, with an eye on the purpose of the meeting, and make sure there's good time to pray. For example, a good meeting might take 10 minutes to warm up, spend 20-30 minutes on the main questions, then 5-10 minutes on extra questions, leaving 20 minutes to pray.

The Spiritual Stuff

What kind of spiritual commitment is it, and what qualities are needed?

- Essentially, sponsoring is about relationship. Your love, honesty and prayerful support will impart to your sponsee what words on paper can't.
- You'll need to get your motives straight. Sponsoring shouldn't be anything to do with wanting to control someone, clone your own personality in them, form a power base of disciples, or seek glory for yourself. However well meaning

we may be, these motives sometimes lurk in the background and need to be confronted. Instead, the aim is simply to serve (see Purpose 3).

- Model the accountability that 4Life suggests, and don't try to take on spiritual responsibility without God's help. This means having your own listening space and pattern of prayer, so that God can strengthen you for the task. It also means making sure you have a sponsor of your own, or some kind of spiritual director or accountability group.
- Be honest. Yes, you are a role model, but it's still OK for you to be you. In fact, this is what will make your meetings powerful. Just be yourself.
- Take the task seriously. Pray for your sponsee daily, read up on 4Life before meetings and think through what might come up. 4Life is a spiritual process, not simply an educational experience or something to talk about. Its power doesn't rest on wise words or theories, but on reading God's word in the Bible and praying together. As you do this, relying on the Holy Spirit, the units will be spiritual dynamite, because God has promised to work through these means - even through you and me (see, for example, Isaiah 55:10-11)
- Learn to listen and share. In every meeting you should be listening more than talking. 'Everyone should be quick to listen, slow to speak' (James 1:19). Your role isn't to lecture or re-teach what the units have already covered. Instead, listen intently to your sponsee, let them take a lead and answer each question as fully as they can, and offer your experiences.

Going Deeper

What are some of the keys to making serious spiritual progress?

- Prayer
- Pay attention to values. 4Life deals with many of the *internal* causes of problems in discipleship. In Identity this might be low self esteem or a poor image of God. In Values, this could be a misunderstanding about Jesus or an overriding need for affection. In Lifestyle it could be the absence of a habit of prayer or any number of unresolved hindrances like unforgiveness. Lastly, in Purpose, it could be a fear of evangelism or lack of experience of the Spirit's power. It's often better to deal with these internal causes, rather than just with the issues in the sponsee's life.
- Lifestyle change has to come from the individual. Remember this, and don't try to do the hard work of discipleship for them. Where appropriate, though, you can encourage action or targets based on what your sponsee has said ('How could you apply that this week?'). Follow up comments and commitments from the previous meeting as the weeks go by (e.g., 'how's the listening space going?').
- Bear in mind the stages of growth: Christian growth begins with *thirst*. Thirst is the desire for God, implanted by the Spirit, that impels us towards Jesus Christ. It can't be manufactured - your job is just to pray for it and watch out for it. Thirsty young Christians can get quite easily frustrated or disappointed

EXTRA

(be ready for this). The second stage is *commitment,* when the rubber hits the road. Before this happens, there may be times of testing, or they may waver for some time (your job, as always, is simply to love and pray them through this). Eventually, real growth is achieved when the selfish values in our lives are replaced by Christ's values, bearing fruit in godly living. This is the aim of 4Life. As far as it depends on you, don't settle for anything less.

Bible Guide

How does the whole Bible story fit together? Think of one Big Story: from creation to new creation. The guide below tells the story in 8 episodes, four from the Old Testament, four from the New Testament. For each episode there are 5 key passages you can read to cover the main headlines of the Bible story and what it means.

The Old Testament

Creation & Fall
God created a wonderful world. He set humans on that world with a unique purpose - to know him and care for his creation. The fall came when selfish humans, beginning with Adam and Eve, rejected God's plans and turned away from him.

Genesis 1:1-2:4a The Universe is created (see Values 1 & Identity 6); Genesis 2:4a-25 Humans and families are created; Genesis 3 The fall and God's judgement on humankind (see Values 2); Genesis 8:13-9:17 God makes a covenant with creation; Psalm 8 Our special place in creation

The Chosen People
Despite all this, God decided to bring his broken creation back to himself, beginning with the chosen people. He chose Abraham and his descendants to be the ones who would know him, be blessed by him, and keep hope alive for the world.

Genesis 12:1-9 God chooses Abram (Abraham) - see Values 3; Genesis 17:1-16 New names and circumcision; Exodus 2:23-3:22 Moses is called by the Lord; Exodus 12:1-16, 29-42 God saves Israel at the Passover; Exodus 20:1-21 The Ten Commandments

The Promised Land
When Abraham's descendants, the Israelites, found themselves as slaves in Egypt, God sent Moses to save them and bring them into the Promised Land. They were called to be a picture of the life God planned for his people. But this never fully happened.

Joshua 24:1-27 Joshua renews the covenant; 1 Samuel 16:1-13 David anointed as King; 2 Samuel 7:1-17 God's promise to David; Psalm 23 David's Song: The Lord is my Shepherd; 2 Chronicles 7:1-6, 11-22 Solomon's Temple

104

Bible Guide

Exile and Return

God's people continued to turn away from him, and so he judged them. Half the nation was deported by Assyria and then the other half was captured by the Babylonians. But God still would not give up. He bought some Israelites back from exile to rebuild Jerusalem and to wait for their destiny to be fulfilled.

Amos 5 Amos prophesies judgement on Israel; 2 Kings 17:1-23 Northern Israel invaded and deported; 2 Chronicles 36:11-23 Judah exiled in Babylon; Jeremiah 31:21-34 A new covenant is promised; Ezra 1:1-4, 3:8-13 Return to Jerusalem

The New Testament

The Kingdom of God

After Israel's exile and return, God sent his Son, Jesus Christ, to save his people and finally bring to pass his plans for the world. Jesus called this the coming of the kingdom of God. Jesus started setting things right: he healed the sick and gave people a new start, and he called disciples to follow him.

John 1:1-14 Jesus: the Word made flesh; Mark 1:14-20 Jesus announces the kingdom (see Values 4); Luke 5:17-26 Who is Jesus?; Matthew 5:1-12 The Beatitudes (see Values 7); Mark 8:27-9:1 The challenge: Who do you say I am? (see Identity 5)

The Cross of Christ

Setting things right would prove more costly still for Jesus. He knew that only if he suffered a rebel's death on the cross would God's rebellious people go free. The cross of Christ is at the heart of the Bible story.

Matthew 26:17-30 The Last Supper; Mark 14:53-65, 15:1-15 Trial and torture; John 19:16-30 Jesus on the cross; Romans 3:21-26 Justified by grace (see Identity 8); Hebrews 2:10-15 Jesus wins victory over Satan

Resurrection and the Church

Because of the cross, the story could continue with Jesus' resurrection and birth of the Church. God raised Jesus from the dead as a sign that all God's people will one day come through death and judgement. But the new life of the church has already started – God sent his Holy Spirit so that his people could live the way they were always meant to live and share with others the good news about Jesus.

Matthew 28:1-20 Resurrection and the great commission (see Values 9); Acts 1:1-11 Jesus ascends to heaven; Acts 2:1-8, 14-24, 36-47 Pentecost and the early church (see Values 9 & Purpose 1); Acts 10:9-35, 44-48 Cornelius – the first Gentile believer; 1 Corinthians 15:20-28 Jesus raised and reigning

The New Creation

Finally, Jesus now reigns with the Father until he completes his work in the new creation. One day all people will rise to be judged, but God will save his people and bring them to live with him in a renewed creation.

Mark 13:1-31 Judgement on Jerusalem and one day on the world; Matthew 24:36-51 Using the time well; Romans 8:18-39 Creation will be released from decay; Revelation 12:1-17 Trials and tribulations for God's people; Revelation 21:1-8, 22-27 The new creation (Values 5)

Habit Breaking

Facing the truth is painful, especially if the truth is that you're struggling with a habit that makes you feel like a failure. But the truth is also liberating. If you're willing to confront the values that drive you (see Values 6-10) and the darker corners of your life (Lifestyle 6-10), God's power will be able to go to work, especially as you share your struggle with one or two other Christians who you can trust. This guide is written out of the experience of struggling to break free. It isn't a list of rules but a set of principles. Whatever it is you struggle with, these 5 scriptural approaches to bad habits should be able to help, even if further prayer and counselling is also needed.

Habits - Bad and Good

"I have heard that allowing a boy to look at pornography just one time can be as addictive as crack cocaine...I have to agree. It is a rush. A young boy with the most innocent of intentions can be drawn in to the trap of sexual addiction. I strongly believe that is what happened to me. I had my first 'hit' of porn, and I was hooked...

...I knew that what I was seeing was dirty, and that made it all the more exciting. I remember my pulse quickening and the adrenaline rushing through my body. At the age of eight, I hadn't felt those things before. They were very foreign feelings. For many years I held the belief that I was the only one who struggled with this sort of thing."

Do you recognise anything here? At first a pattern of behaviour is formed by an early, powerful experience, often before we know what we're getting into. Soon enough a habit is formed and with it feelings of guilt and isolation. Following that, failed attempts to break free lead to even more guilt and a feeling of powerlessness, and the cycle continues. This is the pattern with so many things: gossip, impure thoughts, laziness, over-work, addictions, violence, destructive relationships and so on.

We need to remember that not all habits are bad. God actually made us to be creatures of habit. Good habits, like courtesy or keeping fit, can be beautiful things. The trick is not to give up habits, but to change them. This fits with what we know of the brain. Your brain is made up of 'pathways' formed by repeated behaviour. The reason habits are hard to change is that new pathways need to be made. If you're walking through a woodland, you tend to walk where there's been most traffic - that is, on the paths. Leaving a path means having to forge a new track with every step, and possibly snagging your trousers on some brambles! Our minds are just the same. We need to make a very conscious choice to leave old pathways (comfortable and easy as they are) and deliberately focus on new pathways - new habits - giving ourselves plenty of motivation and support as we do.

None of this is news to God. He's been in the habit of giving his people new habits for millennia. But it does remind us how important the habits of faith are.

Habit Breaking

This is why the book of Deuteronomy recommends a whole set of habits for Israelites to keep their mind on God's law (Deuteronomy 6:4-9). And it's why Paul says to Timothy '*train yourself* to be godly' (1 Timothy 4:7). Does this mean God isn't going to step in and heal you immediately? Not necessarily. It's just that some habits are broken more in our spirits (the deep place only God truly knows), and some are broken in our minds. How God delivers us is his choice, but letting us tackle some of the issues in our minds is part of the way God treats us as free, beloved and dignified children, which is exactly who we are.

ADART – a way of breaking habits

Admit

Therefore confess your sins to each other and pray for each other so that you may be healed. The prayer of a righteous person is powerful and effective.   **James 5:16**

The first step is to admit. Admit the issue to yourself (this can be harder than it sounds, especially if you've been telling yourself 'it's not a problem any more'). Admit it to God, too. Be honest - bring the real you to the real God and the healing can begin. You should probably admit it to someone else, too. Like a wise school nurse caring for a grazed knee, God often insists (despite our protests) that our wounds need to be exposed and cleaned *first,* before the reassuring bandage goes on.

Another part of stage one is to admit that there's a reason behind your habits. As one author wrote, 'they give you a secret pleasure, a special little thrill. They're your unquestioning, unconditional friends'. This is so true, even for habits we hate that ruin our lives, there's some kind of benefit somewhere, a comfort we get or a pain we avoid. It might be 'I eat too much because I can't cope with stress', or 'I get drunk because I want people to think I'm funny', or 'I flirt because it makes me feel wanted'.

- Is it time for you to admit your issue to God?
- You could spend some time thinking and praying about causes and triggers. What caused your habit? Where and why did it begin?
- Also, think about triggers. What triggers your habit? Where and when does it tend to happen? What does it save you from / what does it give you?

Decide

For you have spent enough time in the past doing what pagans choose to do - living in debauchery, lust, drunkenness, orgies, carousing and detestable idolatry.   **1 Peter 4:3**

How much time is enough time? It depends on the issue you're dealing with. Some acts are so serious that we should leave them behind immediately never to return. Others take longer to deal with and, sometimes to our surprise, are lower down on God's priority list than we think. We want to 'conquer all negative thoughts', but God might first want to teach us to pray.

It's also possible that what's on your mind isn't a bad habit to crack, but something else. Think carefully and seek advice: should your love of beer lead to an alcohol-free life, or just more moderation? Is being impetuous something to give up or a personality trait to work with?

Lastly, you need to decide wisely if this is a time when you are ready to put effort into lasting change. Half-hearted changes are more likely to lead to stress, failure and a crushed spirit, so choose your time wisely. There does come a time for decision though, and perhaps that time is now. In that case, having thought it over first, make a resolute decision which you plan to stick to even when perseverance is needed. This seems to be what Job did, 'I made a covenant with my eyes not to look lustfully at a virgin' (Job 31:1).

Ask yourself:

- Is this definitely a bad habit? Is this the time to break it? Are you willing to give it enough priority?
- Are you ready not just to admit your issue, but to repent of it? Even if changing your habits can take some time, you can still turn that corner by saying to God, 'I no longer wish to live this way'
- It may be right to pick a date, get support and go for it. Prepare mentally by listing all the pros and cons of keeping your habit and of giving up. Pick 2-3 positive reasons for giving up to focus on.

Avoid

Like a city whose walls are broken through is a person who lacks self-control. **Proverbs 25:28**

Avoiding the cause of a problem is exactly what Joseph did (Genesis 39:10-12) and what King David didn't (2 Samuel 11:2). First of all, we need to avoid *gateways*. What leads you the action you want to change? Is it when you're Hungry, Angry, Lonely or Tired (HALT)? When 2 or 3 of these are true, we're likely to be tempted and it's time to halt! Are there other causes like drink, late nights, TV, a certain environment, a certain time, or certain people?

Secondly, we need to build *walls*. This could mean removing a cause of temptation or removing *yourself* from the path of temptation. If going to the pub makes you volatile, go there only with certain friends, or set a boundary to leave by a certain time. Putting walls in place means that, even if you break a wall, you've still not actually done anything wrong and there's still time to sort yourself out.

- What are your gateways?
- What walls can you build?
- When you find yourself tempted, learn to pray, or just to verbalise your situation ('OK, so I'm tired, what am I going to do?'). This helps you to take more responsibility for the choices you're making.

Refocus

Finally, brothers, whatever is true, whatever is noble, whatever is right, whatever is pure, whatever is lovely, whatever is admirable - if anything is excellent or praiseworthy - think about such things. Whatever you have learned or received or heard from me, or seen in me - put it into practice. And the God of peace will be with you. **Philippians 4:8-9**

Habit Breaking

No human life is a vacuum - whatever you take out will need to be replaced by something (Matthew 12:43-45). The key is to fill your life with good things by refocusing on what's healthy, enjoyable and worthwhile. Violence can be replaced by sport (depending how it's played!); gossip by prayer; late night TV by reading; swearwords by alternatives; and, sometimes, unhelpful friends by good ones. Refocusing isn't just about filling your life with something *else,* but something *good.* Not only does this make you too busy for your old behaviour, it also boosts your self-esteem, which is useful because feeling low is a cause of bad habits anyway. Occasional treats, good hygiene, more sleep, and a bit of a healthier lifestyle (no need to become Jane Fonda) can increase your confidence and break the shame spiral ('I can't believe I'm so crap, I've failed again, I don't deserve to look after myself...'). Don't believe that rubbish - take a deep breath (or 10!) and say something true to yourself, like 'I am worth looking after, and with God's help I'm going to change'

- What can you refocus your life on?
- What will boost your self-esteem and give you motivation to change?
- Is there anything you can do to find release when you're feeling tempted?
  (Decide in advance that this is what you'll do)

Try Again

Let us not become weary in doing good, for at the proper time we will reap a harvest if we do not give up.   **Galatians 6:9**

Let's say you do fail. What will probably hurt more than anything will be your pride - 'I was going to make it this time, now I'm just a failure'. Refuse the guilt and recrimination (it doesn't help). Instead, confess to God and receive his forgiveness. We all need to learn to be forgiven and forgive ourselves.

We can also learn from our mistakes. Maybe there's something you could have avoided, and that was your lesson. Oscar Wilde had a point, 'the person who succeeds is the one who learns by failure'. But what we learn most from failure isn't tips for success. What we learn most is to cling to God in all our weakness, and this is in fact a more important lesson than any other.

We may, indeed, be sure that perfect chastity - like perfect charity - will not be attained by any merely human efforts. You must ask for God's help. Even when you have done so, it may seem to you for a long time that no help, or less help than you need, is being given. Never mind. After each failure, ask forgiveness, pick yourself up, and try again.

Very often what God first helps us towards is not the virtue itself but just this power of always trying again. For however important chastity (or courage, or truthfulness, or any other virtue) may be, this process trains in us habits of the soul which are more important still. It cures our illusions about ourselves and teaches us to depend on God. We learn, on the one hand, that we cannot trust ourselves even in our best moments, and, on the other, that we need not despair even in our worst, for our failures are forgiven. The only fatal thing is to sit down content with anything less than perfection.   *C. S. Lewis*

Don't let failure drive you away from God - let it draw you to him in weakness. Accept your weakness ('there I go again Lord, I'm so weak unless you help me. Thank you for your grace for someone like me'). And learn one more habit - the

EXTRA

habit of dusting yourself off. Soldiers don't return to their home barracks because of minor falls; they take a moment to steady themselves and get back into the fray. You're still alive; you're still part of God's assault on evil; there's still time.

> There is no single definition of holiness, there are dozens, hundreds. But there is one I am particularly fond of; being holy means getting up immediately every time you fall. It does not mean never falling into sin. It means being able to say, 'yes, Lord, I have fallen a thousand times. But thanks to you I have got up again a thousand and one times'. That's all. I like thinking about that.
> *Archbishop Helder Camara*

Gifts Checklist

Below is a list giving details of the different types of spiritual gifts found in the New Testament. We don't know precisely how all of them work. Some of them sound more natural, some more supernatural. Some people use more than one gift (see Acts 9:10-19), others have a main gift that marks them out. What's certain is this: they're all given through grace by God to help the church. We might think of four kinds of gift – in leadership, in bringing a message, in miracles and in caring. Apart from those groupings, they're not necessarily in any order. Remember, too that the list isn't exhaustive. There are many other gifts or abilities God can use, too: practical skills, hospitality, music, etc...

Gifts of Leadership
Apostleship
Biblical basis: 1 Corinthians 12:28, Ephesians 4:9   Examples: Mark 3:13-19, Acts 4:32-35

In the New Testament, the apostles were the leaders especially sent by Jesus into the world as witnesses of his resurrection (Acts 1:21-22). Sometimes other people are described as apostles (Acts 14:14) - these were people sent for a specific task, such as starting a church in a new city. The original apostles still lead us through their letters in the New Testament. Apostles are pioneers, risk-takers, people on the move. Their faith is strong and wise. They inspire faith in others, they proclaim the message about Jesus and they oversee the development of leaders.

Leading
Biblical basis: Romans 12:8   Example: 1 Thessalonians 5:12-13

Leaders are the ones who take charge or care for the people. The gift of leading enables someone to handle responsibility well - perhaps for one project, or in a 9-5 job, or perhaps as an official leader in the church. Leaders in the church need to be gentle, self-controlled, mature and have a good reputation in the community (see 1 Titus 3:1-7).

Gifts Checklist

Administration
Biblical basis: 1 Corinthians 12:28   Example: Acts 6:1-4

This gift seems to be about giving order and direction to the church, like steering a boat. This kind of leading involves giving guidance, helping to plan and to see those plans come to reality. Administrators will be useful members of teams or church councils.

Gifts in Bringing a Message

Prophecy
Biblical basis: Romans 12:6, 1 Corinthians 12:28, Ephesians 4:11   Examples: Acts 11:27-30, Acts 13:1-3

A prophecy is a message which is revealed to the speaker by God. Paul explained that 'everyone who prophesies speaks to men for their strengthening, encouragement and comfort' (1 Corinthians 14:3). This could mean an encouraging word from God, explaining what some teaching means in practice, or giving a message about the future. Prophecy involves a step of faith by the person sharing it, and a process of testing by the hearers (1 Thessalonians 5:19-22). People who often prophesy will be insightful, proven to hear from God and both encouraging and challenging to those around them.

Teaching
Biblical basis: Romans 12:7, 1 Corinthians 12:28, Ephesians 4:11   Examples: Acts 18:24-26, 2 Timothy 2:2

To teach is to explain the Christian faith and hand on its message. Jesus is the great teacher (Matthew 23:5-8); our job is to pass on his teachings to the world (Matthew 28:18-20). They may well be leaders who have responsibility for instructing others in the church. Teachers have good Bible knowledge, can communicate healthy teaching, and need to have lives that match up to it.

Evangelism
Biblical basis: Ephesians 4:11 Examples: Acts 8:4-8 & 12

Evangelists announce the good news of Jesus Christ. They declare that Christ is Lord and call people to believe in him and be baptised. All Christian teachers need to make this announcement (2 Timothy 4:5), just like all Christians are called to witness to their friends (1 Peter 3:15). But evangelists will be more likely to search out opportunities to share the message and more able to bring friends and other contacts to Christ.

Discernment
Biblical basis: 1 Corinthians 12:10 Examples: 1 Corinthians 14:29, 1 Thessalonians 5:20-21

Discernment is the ability to test prophetic messages and sort out what is helpful from what isn't. We all need to carefully weigh any message in church against the Bible's teaching; but people with the gift of discernment are often able to spot when a message is from God. They may be able to see what gifts others have, too.

Messages of wisdom, knowledge and revelation
Biblical basis: 1 Corinthians 12:8   Examples: 1 Corinthians 14:26

These messages seem to be a bit like prophecy - little impressions, words or pictures. They need to be shared in faith and tested by others, but they can encourage other Christians and build up their faith.

Tongues & Interpreting Tongues
Biblical basis: 1 Corinthians 12:28   Examples: Acts 10:44-46

Tongues is the ability to praise and pray to God in another language. Occasionally, this might be an actual language you don't naturally know how to speak (Acts 2:5-6). But often speaking in tongues won't make sense to anybody. This is why Paul used it in private prayer and said that when tongues are used in public they need to be explained (1 Corinthians 14:13-19). The person who spoke in tongues might do this (1 Corinthians 14:13) or someone else, with the gift of interpretation, might hear from God what the explanation is.

Gifts in Miracles
Miracles
Biblical basis: 1 Corinthians 12:28 Example: Acts 6:8

Nothing is impossible when it comes to asking for things in prayer, but some people have a special gift of miracles. In the book of Acts, this included a supernatural escape from prison and raising someone from the dead (see Acts chapters 12 & 20). This is the power of Jesus at work, producing signs of his kingdom (Ephesians 1:18-21).

Healing
Biblical basis: 1 Corinthians 12:28   Example: Acts 3:1-8

All Christians can pray for healing, especially leaders of the church (James 5:14), but some Christians have a gift of healing. They may feel more of a call to pray for the sick, and will have greater effectiveness when they pray for healing.

Faith
Biblical basis: 1 Corinthians 12:28 Example: Acts 14:8-10

This special gift is given when extra faith is needed to see something unusual or supernatural come to pass. We all have saving faith in Jesus, but this is faith for something in particular. People with this gift will find themselves able to believe that incredible things can happen by God's power.

Gifts in Caring
Pastoring
Biblical basis: Ephesians 4:11 Examples: See Ezekiel 34:1-6, John 21:15-17

The Biblical picture of a pastor is a shepherd. It refers to those who care for and guide the people of God. Someone with a pastoral gift may be a leader and teacher (see 1 Peter 5:1-4), but they could also be a person with a genuine concern for the welfare of other Christians. Pastors will be those who naturally counsel, encourage and listen to others, with sensitivity to what is appropriate at the right time.

Helping

Biblical basis: 1 Corinthians 12:28 Examples: Acts 20:35, Romans 16:1-2

This could refer to any kind of assistance - from hospitality (Romans 12:13), to visiting prisoners (Hebrews 13:3) and caring for those who suffer (Matthew 25:35-36). Helpers are lead by the heart, but they are also able to get things done. They look at people and situations with eyes to see where people might be in need, and they see their home, their time and their possessions as ways to show God's love.

Serving

Biblical basis: Romans 12:7 Examples: Acts 6:1-4, Acts 11:29-30, 1 Corinthians 16:15

The word Paul uses for this is often used for ministry or the work of the church. Serving could be helping with the running of the church, caring for needy Christians or taking on a job that needs doing. No Christian is exempt from the call to serve (Purpose 3) but those with a gift of serving may have a more practical mindset, getting on quietly with what needs to be done and paying attention to necessary details.

Showing Mercy

Biblical basis: Romans 12:8 Examples: Matthew 18:23-35, Luke 10:30-37

All of us must be merciful (Matthew 5:7) but certain Christians will have a naturally merciful heart. Their compassion will inspire them to acts of forgiveness and to sacrifices for the sake of others. They may be less likely to judge others and have a strong sense of God's concern for the poor.

Encouraging

Biblical basis: Romans 12:8 Examples: Acts 4:36-37 & 11:22-24, 1 Thessalonians 3:1-3

To encourage is to come alongside someone and spur them on. Encouragers may not initially recognise this gift in themselves as it operates naturally and gently. But they can be spotted by what they leave behind them - a trail of inspired, uplifted and valued people. They are vital in any cell or team as they preserve hope.

Contributing to others

Biblical basis: Romans 12:8, 1 Corinthians 13:3 Examples: Romans 15:25-27

The responsibility to give applies to anyone who is blessed by God with wealth (1 Timothy 6:17-19). Those with the gift of giving, though, will also be eager to give no matter how much they have in the bank (2 Corinthians 8:1-5). They tend to see money as an opportunity to invest in the kingdom of God and learn, perhaps more quickly than others, to hold their finances loosely.

Other Resources

Help! I'm leading part of my cell meeting
by Trevor Withers
This booklet is for cell members leading one of the 4Ws. If your heart sinks when it's your turn to lead part of your cell meeting, this booklet is for you. It aims to give members confidence as they participate in the cell meeting. Presenting the key components needed to make each of the 4Ws run effectively, it offers practical advice and ideas which will stimulate cell members' creativity and enhance their leadership abilities.

Simply Cell
By Laurence Singlehurst, Liz West and Trevor Withers
What it stays on the cover is what this book is about. It explains cell in a dynamic yet simple way. Suitable for anyone about to join a cell whether they are from Alpha or existing church members who are new to cell. This booklet will also encourage long-term cell people.

Equipping Future Cell Leaders
by Liz West and Trevor Withers
This course has been designed to equip leaders to do more than lead a structure cell meeting. It is developed from the values base of the cell model and is an opportunity to establish the plumbline of cell for the new cell leaders.

Evangelism through Cells
by Laurence Singlehurst and Liz West
Loving people and reaching out is what we know we should do – but do we? This booklet contains practical strategies on how to reach out as individuals and groups and demonstrates how cells can encourage and empower us all to love the lost. This booklet is for church leaders, cell supervisors and cell leaders who want to be mobilised as workers in the harvest and who want to lead others to become workers too.

Other Resources

Loving the Lost
by Laurence Singlehurst
From his experience of working with numerous churches in the
UK as they look at the cell church idea, Laurence Singlehurst
explores the principles and practice of cell church. He works from
basic definitions and values to practical application. A key focus
is the area of evangelism through the cell church model.

Life in His Body
By David Finnell
A simple guide to active cell life. Life in His Body is practical,
simple and comprehensive. It synthesises the inner workings of a
cell church. It clearly communicates the keys to a vital cell-based
church: prayer community, team evangelism, servant leadership
and vision. Throughout are lively questions and strategies, which
illustrate these components. Communicate the vision of cells to
everyone in your church with this simple tool.

Easy ways to place your order:
phone: 01582 463330 or e-mail
cellukresources@oval.com
Or for a full list of resources visit:
www.celluk.org.uk
Payment may be made by credit card or invoice.
Postage and packing will be charged extra.

Cell UK also offer a range of training opportunities
and conferences. For current information browse our
website at:
www.celluk.org.uk

About the Author

Mark is married to Ailsa and has two boys, Jonah and Zach. He has been a theology student, secondary school teacher and curate, and he is now an Associate Pastor at St. Paul's Hammersmith. Mark is a founding friend of Breathe, a Christian network for simpler living (www.ibreathe.org.uk).